Citizen of the World

Citizen of the World

Suffering and Solidarity in the Twenty-First Century

By
Donald H. Dunson and
James A. Dunson III

ORBIS BOOKS
Maryknoll, New York 10545

ORBIS BOOKS
Maryknoll, New York 10545

Fathers and Brothers
MARYKNOLL™

Founded in 1970, Orbis Books endeavors to publish works that enlighten the mind, nourish the spirit, and challenge the conscience. The publishing arm of the Maryknoll Fathers and Brothers, Orbis seeks to explore the global dimensions of the Christian faith and mission, to invite dialogue with diverse cultures and religious traditions, and to serve the cause of reconciliation and peace. The books published reflect the views of their authors and do not represent the official position of the Maryknoll Society. To learn more about Maryknoll and Orbis Books, please visit our website atwww.maryknollsociety.org.

Library of Congress Cataloging-in-Publication Data

Dunson, Donald H.
    Citizen of the world : suffering and solidarity in the 21st century / by Rev. Donald H. Dunson and Dr. James A. Dunson III.
        pages cm
    Includes bibliographical references and index.
    ISBN 978-1-62698-045-7 (pbk.)
    1. Compassion—Religious aspects—Christianity.   2. Charity—Religious aspects—Christianity.   3. Solidarity—Religious aspects—Christianity.   I. Dunson, James A., III.   II. Title.

BV4647.S9D86 2013
261.8—dc23

2013021157

For Mrs. Mary Bulger, a true friend and lifelong learner. Mizpah.

Contents

Acknowledgments

Writing this book has been an adventure. We are especially grateful for the gracious hospitality of four different religious communities:

The Congregation of the Sisters of the Sacred Heart in northern Uganda, led by our friend, Sr. Rosemary, opened their hearts and home to us in 2001. Ever since, their community at St. Monica's Girls' Tailoring Center has felt like our African home.

The Jesuit Community of Brothers and Priests in Mumbai, India, welcomed us to share in their life and ministry in 2011. They enabled us to have access to people and experiences in their homeland we could never have known without their generous assistance. Father Alex Colaco's boundless energy kept us on the move toward new discoveries.

The Irish Christian Brothers at St. Mary's School on Dum Dum Street in Kolkata, India, provided us with warm hospitality in the quarters above their school. We have great memories of tasty evening meals with lively conversations that marked the end of each of our days in their company.

The Benedictine Community of St. Joseph Abbey in Covington, Louisiana, has been a place of quiet reflection for us. Our good friend Abbot Justin Brown is the embodiment of southern hospitality.

Finally, Donald Sempa, our Ugandan son and brother, led us through his beautiful country, accompanied us to India, and offered invaluable insights and suggestions for the manuscript.

Introduction

In 1990, the spacecraft Voyager I was passing Saturn on its celebrated journey through the solar system. The astronomer Carl Sagan suggested to NASA scientists that, after completing its mission, they ought to spin the spacecraft around until it was facing in the direction of home—the tiny planet Earth—and take a snapshot from the greatest distance from home that we have yet explored. From so vast a distance, the Earth appears inconsequential, a tiny dot that is easily lost in a huge array of stars and planets. Sagan was deeply moved by this image and commented: "This distant image of our tiny world . . . underscores our responsibility to deal more kindly with one another, and to preserve and cherish the pale blue dot, the only home we have ever known."[1]

Sagan's prescient observations are our own. Yes, the earth is our only home, and bonds of kinship mysteriously bond us to all seven billion human beings who call our small planet home. To deal more kindly with one another is likely the sole path to a more hopeful future for all of humanity. We are not naïve about the powerful forces that militate against this, but we all have reason to be hopeful in this present moment that holds so much promise.

Sister Helen Prejean, the author of *Dead Man Walking*, once noted that there are two situations that can give birth to a fascinating storyteller: either an extraordinary person plunges into the commonplace, or an ordinary person gets caught up in incredible, astonishing experiences. The latter has certainly been our experience. We are two ordinary persons, bonded by family ties to each other and connected by our common experience of being eyewitnesses to some of humanity's most crushing burdens and the people forced to bear them. Ours is also the experience of seeing up close the resilience and joy in the faces of those who possess practically nothing in this world but an unbreakable bond of solidarity with others. We share the moral conviction that it is possible to fashion a more just and humane world, and together we have been exploring possible avenues to arrive at that aim.

Allow us at the outset to share some of our personal and professional background. We have been raised in the same family in different generations. In our home, civic virtue was paramount. Even in childhood we could sense the pride our parents took in sacrificing out of their love for family and community. Don became a Catholic priest at age twenty-six. He studied for seven years in the medieval city of Louvain in the heart of Belgium. For the last two decades Don taught moral theology at St. Mary Seminary in Cleveland, Ohio. He now serves as pastor at St. Vincent DePaul Church in Elyria, Ohio. He continues to focus on fundraising for the St. Kizito Foundation, a charity he founded to fund primary and secondary school education in Uganda. In 2008 Jim received his PhD in philosophy from Emory University in Atlanta. He has taught a wide variety of courses in philosophy and political science, focusing especially on the history of philosophy and ethics. Jim is currently an assistant professor of philosophy at Xavier University of Louisiana in New Orleans.

We have been blessed to journey far and wide across the globe, sometimes separately and sometimes together. We have seen children at play in many of Africa's villages and in the streets of Mumbai. We have gathered at the tomb of Mother Teresa in Kolkata. We have befriended young people in El Salvador who have never stepped foot in a school. In Kenya we joined with volunteers from around the world to care for young boys and girls who have seen both their mothers and fathers die of AIDS. We have listened intently to the stories of those who live in pockets of deep poverty in the United States, desperately poor in a land of plenty.

It is hard to know which memory is more enduring: the profound and unmet needs of the countless people across the globe that we have encountered, most especially the children, or the extraordinary sense of pride, hospitality, and hope exhibited by those same people. We were frequently astonished by the resolve and resourcefulness of the extremely vulnerable people we met.

This book is many years in the making. However, as is often the case when writing about one's travels and experiences, its deeper meaning was not clear until we had time for reflection and the chance to ponder the significance of what we experienced. In the summer of 2001 we ventured together to Africa for the first time. This trip led to Don's first book, *No Room at the Table: Earth's Most Vulnerable Children.* That book documents the plight of AIDS orphans, homeless children and refugees, child soldiers, and the millions of persons still suffering from chronic hunger and malnourishment. In the summer of 2011, a decade after our first trip to Africa, we both came to the realization that something vital was missing from our experience. Neither of us had ever stepped foot on earth's most populated continent: Asia. We resolved to travel together to India, along with our friend from Uganda, Donald Sempa.

After this eye-opening trip, we each set about writing a series of reflections that eventually coalesced into this larger project. Our collaboration has produced a manuscript that offers two distinct perspectives on our shared travels and many experiences. It is clearly composed of two different parts, one more narrative and theological (Don) and the other more reflective and philosophical (Jim). At stake are the following questions: What does it really mean to be a citizen of the world, how might we better become one, and what serious constraints inhibit our ability to do so?

Don's part of the book focuses our attention on how we ought to regard, ideally, our obligations to people half a world away. It grounds this ideal in lived experience and provides concrete examples of solidarity in action. Don's passion for telling the extraordinary stories of ordinary people has fueled thirty years of homilies. Jim's part investigates the meaning of this ideal, rigorously examining its basic presuppositions and wondering about its practical limitations. It places the ideas of solidarity and global citizenship within the broader context of the history of Western philosophy and social thought. It also incorporates real-life examples to better understand these abstract ideas.

While we agree that we should strive to become citizens of the world, we offer different perspectives on this ideal. Jim's philosophical reflections begin each chapter, and Don's theologically based narratives are included at the end of each chapter. The afterword is a shared attempt at bringing together these two approaches. Our hope is that these two approaches might, despite their differences, be fruitfully read as two important perspectives on the same issue.

Notes

[1] Carl Sagan, *Pale Blue Dot* (New York: Random House, 1994), 7.

Chapter 1

A New Citizen for a New World

I am not an Athenian or a Greek, but a citizen of the world.

—Diogenes of Sinope

Jim

In a scene from the popular TV show *The Office*, a youth ministry leader gives a speech to her congregation before the group leaves for a mission trip to Mexico. She enthusiastically describes the difficult task that lay ahead of them, making the following comment: "My parents explained it to me this way. You wouldn't hesitate to save a family member from a burning building, but what if the earth was your building and all the people on it were your family?" Andy, a character on the show, whispers the following to his table of co-workers: "What if the moon was your car and Jupiter was your hairbrush?" Admittedly, the joke is more absurd than it is funny. But might we learn something from such a question? After all, only a small fraction of people who have ever lived would actually grasp the meaning of her analogy. Undoubtedly an even smaller percentage of people would comprehend her claim in such a way that it would motivate a change in their lives. At stake is the question of what it means to be a citizen of the world.

Although the idea that one might be a citizen of the world is an ancient one, the actual ability to follow through on obligations to others whom we will never meet is a recent development in

our increasingly globalized world. Disasters like the tsunami in
Japan and the earthquake in Haiti have prompted an unprecedented amount of charitable contributions worldwide. Governments, nongovernmental organizations (NGOs), and aid groups
like the Red Cross and UNICEF have all, to a greater or lesser
degree, concerned themselves with helping those in need across
the world. For a more personal experience, one might consider
the Peace Corps. Or, for those unable to make that kind of commitment, a typical vacation could easily turn into a rewarding
experience of volunteering. An international excursion might
give you jetlag for a few days, but at least it won't take months to
get where you want to go. While ancient philosophers pondered
the idea of being a citizen of the world, people today can take
practical steps toward actually accomplishing it.

And yet, in spite of the promise of increased solidarity worldwide, we do not always follow through with our commitments
to others. There is a crucial difference between pledging money
and actually delivering it. Once it is delivered, it must be used
wisely. Unfulfilled promises to tsunami victims and an epidemic
of mismanaged money in Haiti call into question the practical results of our new identity as world citizens.[1] Or consider
the UN Rio Earth Summit in 1992. The extraordinary promises made by developed nations were subsequently, and almost
unanimously, broken. More than twenty years later, major world
leaders continue to preach the importance of sustainable development, but noble claims all too often turn into hot air.

To make matters even more complicated, we often fail to ask
hard questions about the foreign aid that accomplishes exactly
what it was supposed to. Consider the examples of Uganda in the
1990s and present-day Zimbabwe. President Yoweri Museveni of
Uganda started a devastating war by invading the Democratic
Republic of Congo in 1998. According to an article in Britain's
The Telegraph, "Uganda could only fund this military campaign
because outsiders were willing to pay such a big share of the
nation's bills. Inadvertently and indirectly, foreign donors ended
up subsidising a conflict that laid waste to Congo. With hindsight,
it would have been better for Africa if Uganda had not received a

penny of foreign aid."[2] This foreign aid no doubt relieved much suffering. However, it had the truly regrettable side effect of enabling a violent man to wage war. The same article notes that Britain has subsidized Zimbabwe's public hospitals and schools to the tune of millions of dollars. While this has certainly benefited the people of Zimbabwe, it has also freed up its brutal dictator, Robert Mugabe, to fund his own lavish lifestyle. Helping those in need, it turns out, is not so morally simple and straightforward *even when it works.*

While we have the opportunity to become personally involved more than ever before, for the most part, we decide not to. Or, to the extent that we make the effort to help others around the world, we impersonally open our checkbooks without calling into question our own identity and without truly investigating the nature of our obligation to others. How could this be, especially when many of us would acknowledge that justice, and not merely charity, calls for us to become involved? In other words, many of us would morally blame a person who had a chance to save a life but didn't, instead of excusing his or her inaction by saying that intervening is optional. Charity is often regarded as gratuitous; it would be nice to help others, but it might not be morally required. Matters of justice, on the other hand, demand our attention and action. Justice delivers what is owed to people, rather than what would be nice to give.

Even if foreign aid is a matter of justice instead of charity, how can we avoid causing more harm by treating other nations paternalistically? In other words, if the poor are owed a certain standard of living, how can this be achieved without regarding them as childlike, passive recipients of help from other countries? A good example is a case of administering justice to a long-oppressed group in the United States. During the era of Reconstruction after the Civil War, the government had to determine how best to incorporate freed slaves into American life.[3] The great African American philosopher and sociologist W. E. B. DuBois (1868–1963) later pointed out the difficulty of offering reparations for injustice while also regarding the recipients as autonomous human beings. The extraordinary challenge facing the nation at that time was how to aid freed slaves without producing "wards of the state."[4] Education was the ultimate goal for DuBois; he praised liberal arts education, because it fostered actual thinking and self-development over rote learning. Still, the challenge of freeing an oppressed group mentally and not just physically was a daunting challenge, especially when it would have required a leap from enslavement to DuBois's ideal of self-development.

The history of colonialism presents a similar dilemma internationally. European forays into Africa (e.g., the Belgian conquest of the Congo[5]) have no doubt contributed to the legacy of corruption and mismanagement of resources that continues in Africa to this day. Difficult questions arise when one considers the morality of ongoing foreign aid to developing countries. At what point does one risk creating a culture of dependence in the country receiving the international aid? Wouldn't this cause even more harm in the long run when the aid money dries up? If the aid is conditional in any way, does this policy in fact promote paternalism on an international scale?

Even in cases of personal charitable contributions, it might matter whether I donate the money for the tax write-off or because I have genuinely experienced a change in my consciousness. If this observation seems too unrealistic and even sanctimonious, it is worth reminding ourselves that we could simply speak in terms of cash instead of promoting ideas like solidarity. But that is not, in fact, how many of us characterize our international obligations.

Despite all the moral and practical difficulties of becoming a citizen of the world, this idea has doubtlessly influenced the world in profound ways. People who embrace this idea often do so with a religious fervor. Aside from moving some people to donate and volunteer, this idea has a unique and uncanny ability to overcome partisan politics. One example is the Clinton-Bush Haiti Fund: tragedy unites once-bitter rivals. The idea of world citizenship has been codified in the UN Declaration of Human Rights, used as justification for military and humanitarian intervention, and presupposed by advocates of controversial institutions like the International Criminal Court (ICC). The very existence of the ICC depends upon the claim that countries do not have final sovereign authority over the prosecution of their indicted citizens. Supporters of the court argue that alleged criminals can be charged, extradited, and tried internationally. In this view, crime knows no borders.

That such an influential idea should be so poorly understood, then, is surprising. The very idea of a citizen of the world sounds contradictory, since "citizen" typically evokes a local, not international, identity. The concept assumes that we share something more substantial than our common humanity. We consider ourselves citizens of a community, city, culture, or country. Understandably, we tend to feel more emotionally bonded with a local community than a nation, since we have daily face-to-face interactions with the people around us. Still, patriotic sentiment and, at the very least, a shared set of rights and obligations enable us to have a more expansive national identity. Compared to the common understanding of the word "citizen," then, the idea of our shared humanity seems a thin thread indeed.

Examining the origins of this idea might offer some insight into its meaning, which can be traced back to the cosmopolitan views of the Cynics and Stoics.[6] The meaning of the word "cosmopolitanism" has changed significantly over time. Nowadays it evokes a person who is well-traveled and appreciates high culture. The original meaning, though, did not carry these high-class or even elitist connotations. Rather, the Cynics and Stoics tried to live simply, according to nature and their own rational insight rather than convention and social norms. The Stoics were much more interested in cultivating social bonds than the Cynics were, but the Cynics also thought of themselves as citizens not just of a society but of a shared world.

The Cynic Diogenes of Sinope (404–323 BCE) was arguably the first citizen of the world, the founding father of cosmopolitanism.[7] He was infamous for his antisocial behavior and for his attempt to justify it philosophically. Like other Cynics, Diogenes wanted to live according to nature instead of being governed by the laws and customs of society. He regarded these laws and customs as deeply unnatural and artificial, so he did not accept their authority. His critics, ancient and modern, dismiss him as the embodiment of a sham ideal: Being a citizen of the world is really a cover for being a citizen of nowhere and an invitation to obey no law but one's own whim. In other words, unlike the standard idea of a citizen, Diogenes' conception of citizenship does not entail a fixed and public set of responsibilities.[8]

The Stoics might be better cosmopolitan role models, since they tried to balance their allegiance to society with cosmopolitan commitments. Perhaps the most famous Stoic, the Roman emperor Marcus Aurelius, fought bravely on the frontlines instead of lounging on the throne.[9] He was deeply patriotic in spite of his cosmopolitanism. But the Stoic defense of cosmopolitanism was also a response to a specific set of social and political circumstances (i.e., the expansion of the Roman Empire into lands occupied by foreigners). With the expansion of the empire, Romans had to reassess their relationships with strangers from strange lands. They had to conceive of a new sort of civic identity that did not depend upon their status as Romans. The idea of a citizen of the world, then, was arguably less a sacred moral ideal than a politically expedient belief.

Much of the literature on this subject either presupposes that cosmopolitanism is the right model of citizenship without addressing whether and how it is possible, or it rejects this model in favor of a patriotic view that affirms local and small-scale obligations. The cosmopolitan view asserts that local and small-scale obligations, while genuine, do not capture the proper scope of our moral obligations. The prominent ethicist Peter Singer, for instance, insists that geography is not a morally relevant fact. We have the ability like never before to help those in need halfway around the world, and it follows that we have the obligation to do so.[10] Kwame Anthony Appiah, another influential ethicist, takes a more refined approach to the question of cosmopolitan citizenship. He emphasizes the challenges it poses, reminding us that we make decisions based on our own subjective experience and not on some abstract moral ideal. Still, he accepts the basic premise that we can be citizens of the world.[11]

Other philosophers like Alasdair MacIntyre challenge the very idea itself, reminding us that citizenship assumes some degree of affective bonds between individuals.[12] The cosmopolitan view asserts an abstract ideal that is at best empty, and at worst an invitation to rationalize all sorts of morally questionable decisions. For instance, it could be used as justification for foreign intervention on the grounds that we have an obligation to people half a world away. But the character of this intervention depends entirely on the specific case. While intervening to prevent genocide and declaring war preemptively are quite different actions, the abstract ideal of cosmopolitanism can easily be manipulated to serve political goals and justify all manner of such actions. And for every high-minded defense of international institutions like the United Nations and the ICC, there are occasional reminders that these organizations are run by human beings with political commitments and biases.

Consider, for instance, the role that the United Nations has played in the history of modern war. Its supporters would argue that it has held countries accountable like never before, acting as an international check on militarist tendencies. In order for an invasion to be regarded as legitimate by the international community, a case typically has to be made at the United Nations. On the other hand, its critics would allege that the United Nations is united in name only and that UN approval is really just a thin cover for the will and interests of one or a few countries. President Harry Truman prudently used the United Nations during the Korean Conflict: technically speaking, it was the "United Nations Joint Command" helping South Korea fight the North. In reality, though, the United States supplied roughly 90 percent of the military force. And a coalition of the willing might have invaded Iraq in 1993, but it is legitimate to ask whether this effort was truly international.

This does not necessarily mean that the United States was wrong in 1950 or 1993. Still, it is worth noting that the United Nations lent credibility to the effort to repel North Korea and Iraq, even though, in the case of Korea, the US Congress was never asked for an official declaration of war. On one hand, the United

Nations establishes a process that makes war subject to formal scrutiny. On the other hand, it makes it easier for world leaders to fight wars informally and by a kind of proxy that makes conflict seem genuinely international.

Some strong arguments might exist for acting like a citizen of the world without genuinely becoming one. For instance, international aid might be one way of projecting power and influence abroad, especially in areas that could become breeding grounds for threats to national security. Assisting poorer countries economically might help to create new trade partners. But neither of these reasons seems genuinely cosmopolitan. They are grounded in prudence and the strategic pursuit of self-interest, rather than the sense of solidarity that the cosmopolitan ideal seems to imply. Doesn't the cosmopolitan ideal require that one raise more than just money? Doesn't it, in fact, imply a change in one's self-understanding? And if raising consciousness is required in addition to raising cash, how is that possible? Merely affirming an abstract ideal does not help us to determine what the ideal would look like in practice.

One source of confusion is the reality that the idea of a citizen of the world is more normative than descriptive. In other words, it is less a statement about what we are than an ideal for which we should strive. The citizen-of-the-world concept helps to expand the scope of our obligation to others, allowing us to move beyond the confines of mere tradition and even serious prejudice. The abolitionist movement in the United States was a cosmopolitan challenge to the belief that racial differences were fundamental. This movement, while often extreme in its methods, promoted the radical equality of individuals and found justification in a specific set of Christian commitments. In another realm, the Catholic Church (as a universal church by the very definition of the word "catholic") has, along with many other Christian denominations, served as a powerful advocate for social justice issues. These churches have as part of their inspiration prominent biblical examples (e.g., the parable of the Good Samaritan) that speak to the obligations we have to total strangers.[13]

On the other hand, perhaps this idea blinds us to the reality of local obligations and the need to cultivate specific traditions. MacIntyre points out that cosmopolitanism is hostile toward specific traditions and ways of life, since these form group bonds by being exclusive rather than inclusive of everyone. But this hostility is disingenuous, because all abstract ideals depend upon such traditions for their content and motivating force. In order for cosmopolitanism to be anything but a set of nice-sounding but empty phrases, some specific customs and habits have to be established that make the idea real. All customs and habits are inevitably going to be local rather than international in character. Even if everyone agreed that being a citizen of the world was possible and desirable, the way people pursue this ideal is determined, at least in part, by where they live.

Different traditions might pursue a cosmopolitan ethic in a variety of ways. Consider, for instance, the different cosmopolitan impulses of an evangelical Christian and an NGO. The character of their efforts will be quite different, so much so that the groups might criticize each other as having misinterpreted the meaning of "cosmopolitanism." For the cosmopolitan ideal to survive, however, it must be possible to defend it outside of a religious context. How could it claim a universal appeal unless its rationale made sense in a wide variety of sacred and secular contexts? This point is especially relevant if being a citizen of the world is more a matter of justice than charity. If it is a matter of justice, then the obligation is strict, and we all (religious and otherwise) are responsible for pursuing it as a moral goal. Its existence as an obligation would not depend on the personal convictions and occasional kindness of potential donors.

As the renowned German philosopher Immanuel Kant (1724–1804) famously claimed, morality must be categorical (or universal, applying to everyone) and an imperative (a command rather than a suggestion).[14] Kant, in fact, was a main inspiration behind the formulation of a Universal Declaration of Human Rights. His idea of cosmopolitan law is a defense of the ties that are unseen, an affirmation of our common humanity.[15] Although he was Christian, his religious beliefs did not determine the kinds of universal ethical obligations he insisted we have to one another.

How, then, can we develop, defend, and promote this cosmopolitan ideal across cultural and religious lines? In chapter 2 and chapter 3, we examine two very different strategies: moral argument and empathy (appeals to the head and appeals to the heart, respectively). Can our obligation to others halfway around the world be argued for in a way that genuinely motivates us to act? What are the benefits and potential problems of an approach that makes me upset or even outraged about suffering that often goes unnoticed? A third promising strategy, discussed in chapter 4, is also available to defenders of the cosmopolitan ideal: appeals to personal experience. Maybe solidarity is possible only after someone has personally experienced one of the dire situations in the world today. Personal experience seems to solve the problems of the first two approaches: it is more convincing than an abstract argument, and meaningful experiences can establish intimate bonds without being emotionally manipulative.

Still, my own experience of visiting Africa and India over the past decade suggests that this approach faces a serious philosophical challenge. A life stirred up inevitably begins to settle, and the hope that one will see the world in a new way must face the reality of habit and routine. Even if a transformation occurs for a few weeks, how long can one actually sustain an active appreciation for what one has experienced? Defenders of a cosmopolitan ideal frequently ignore these challenges, undermining their own case by refusing to ask how we can sustain the deep bonds upon which solidarity depends.

In the following chapters we discuss these three strategies with the hope of better understanding their merits and their weaknesses. Our working assumption is that many people believe that we do and, in fact, have some sort of obligation to people half a world away. The question, then, is how it is possible not just to accept but to *sustain* an appreciation for the ties that bind, especially when those ties are invisible? After discussing these three strategies, we outline several steps one might take toward becoming a citizen of the world. By thinking more carefully about this concept we can better appreciate the challenge, as well as the possibility, of adopting this kind of self-understanding.

Finally, we consider the extent to which we are responsible for and can limit the ordinary suffering that is rampant in the world.

Don

The children I've encountered in East Africa love to give nicknames. They've given me three nicknames over the last decade. Each is a name I would never have chosen for myself. At first, I was called *muzungu*, literally, "white man." Second, I was called "fat man." In a land where so many are rail-thin, I appeared to others as "prosperous" and "well fed," or in the words of the kids, fat. My third nickname on this continent where half the population is under the age of fifteen is "old man." White man, fat man, old man: unflattering names perhaps, but names that made me consider what the world looks like to these young, thin, black-skinned youths. While I appear very different from them in age, culture, and looks, there is clearly a strong bond of humanity between us. The superficial differences between us pale in comparison.

One of the most powerfully unifying forces in the human story has always been food. The sharing of food brings together families and communities. A dark part of the human story is that food both unites us and tears us apart. No more terrifying division exists among us than that which divides those who have enough to eat and those who do not.

In the village of Atiak in northern Uganda, the children are hungry. Five straight seasons of crop failures have forced these young people into the swelling ranks of our sisters and brothers across the globe now suffering the punishing effects of hunger. At the height of the world's financial crisis in 2008 and 2009, an astonishingly large number of people, perhaps as many as 100 million, fell into food insecurity. In 2009, slightly over 1 billion people throughout the world suffered from the scourge of hunger, one-sixth of all humanity.[16] Globally, we have been moving slowly and silently toward an unprecedented peril caused by hunger. At the same time, far too many of us remain unfamiliar with hunger's human face.

The day of my first visit to Atiak, I was heartbroken by devastating news from the local pastor. Two children from the parish were being buried that very morning. Father Arnold related to me how their families had been enduring food scarcity for months on end. These two youths came across some cassava that was spoiled. Cassava is a major staple food in much of Africa, providing the basic diet for around 500 million people around the world. Even though the cassava didn't look right or taste normal, empty stomachs can prompt desperate risks. The children ate the cassava, the last thing they would eat.

Though humanity was born in Africa, its people today are young. In the majority of Africa's fifty-four nations, half of the entire population is under fifteen years old. While remaining spirited and spontaneous, there is still a vacant and detached look in the eyes of these children that so often accompanies hunger. Millions of Africa's young people do not sense that they are in any way important to the future of humanity. An untold number have been told subtly that they have no room at the table. They have been erroneously led to believe that their future is to die young and be quickly forgotten. They sense that there is not food enough, medicine enough, or love enough for all humanity to share, and that, regrettably, some must go without. No child of God should ever be deceived in this way.

No matter where my travels lead me I can predict the most compelling sights I am likely to see—all in the faces of the people I encounter. The French philosopher Emmanuel Levinas spent his entire lifetime developing what has come to be called a "philosophy of the face."[17] Levinas proposes that there is an ethical appeal that we discover only in the face of the other. Its demand is immediately and intuitively known. In gazing upon the face of the other we can discover the radical unity that exists within our one human family. The other's face is not an object merely to see, but pure expression: defenseless and revealing. Levinas speaks of the face of the other who is widow, orphan, and stranger. Each one of these lacks something essential: spouse, parents, home. Indeed, we are all incomplete. Something is lacking in each one of us, and our completion is bound up in our discovery of another.

Levinas's insights probe deeply into how our existence is profoundly related to that of others, for better or worse. The other is part of me in an undeniable and unavailable way that calls out to be recognized and embraced. In our era, increasingly pervaded by a radicalized individualism, this worldview brings to light the hidden moral attachments we have to all others. In opening ourselves to discover the face of the other, we also encounter our true identity.

Volunteering at a Ugandan orphanage I witnessed an African child exhibit an act of solidarity and generosity that is forever etched in my memory. Nearly 150 boys, ages five to fifteen, live together in this orphanage under the watchful care of Salesian priests and brothers. One Sunday afternoon I attended a sports competition. On a whim I decided to offer a Snickers bar as a prize. The children rarely, if ever, get chocolate. Two boys tied for first place, splitting the one candy bar in half. Then I watched as one of them shared his prize with fifteen friends. All of his friends lined up. He extended the prize to them, and each took a speck of chocolate. In the end, nothing remained in this youngster's hand. He had never tasted chocolate, and when the opportunity presented itself he shared everything with his companions. His action that day reminded me that some people only know one way to give: with both hands, with all their heart, without a second thought. That night I couldn't sleep. I stayed awake reflecting on this act of generosity and wondering what I might have done if I were that boy. What I know for certain is that, before I die, I want to become a person who so naturally shows such magnanimity and generosity as that noble boy did.

When I return to that moment in prayer, I cannot help but contrast the way I give to others out of my own abundance with the generosity of this boy who possesses practically nothing. Parents and teachers had taught me self-reliance as well as altruism. In numerous, subtle ways it was inculcated in me that I must be proactive in securing my own needs and desires. After that, I would be expected to reach out to others in an act of gratitude for all that I had. This Ugandan child's stunning yet simple act of generosity inverted the order I had always followed. He placed others first, ahead of himself. Such self-surrender requires a whole worldview in which we trust in providence for attention to our needs. There is, then, a freedom to let another's life be as vital and important as our own.

At that same orphanage I experienced physical hunger once to a degree I had never known before or since. While working in Uganda my schedule is generally less demanding, and the overall pace of life is slower. But one day I was extremely occupied and missed out on the meals served. Then, the following day, I again missed breakfast and lunch. Supper was being served very late, and I hadn't eaten in almost two days. As I stood in line with the boys awaiting the chance to eat, I felt an irritation brought on by hunger. At that point I blurted out the words, "I'm starving here!"

I have used the word "starvation" casually since childhood. I would use it to persuade my mother of my desperate need for her homemade chocolate-chip cookies. In Uganda, however, starvation is used to mean a hunger unto death. After hearing my rather desperate cry, a rail-thin ten-year-old boy approached me to offer his comfort. He started rubbing my belly and calling out to me with a sense of hopefulness in his voice, "No, no, look here" (pointing at my belly), "you have reserves, you have reserves!" This child opened my eyes to a reality that has always been present in my life without ever being consciously and deliberately acknowledged: my food security. I have always known food and drink in steady supply.

The night I saw my young Ugandan friend share his prize with others to the point of self-sacrifice occurred in July 2011. In my reflections that followed daily from that event, I was drawn, in my imagination, to a time precisely seventy years earlier, to July 1941. The place was Auschwitz. The principal player in the unfolding drama that played in my mind and heart was Maximilian Kolbe.[18] Instead of the young boys running around the compound at the Children and Life Mission at Namugongo, I saw weakened men in striped convict garments, each with an emaciated look in his eyes. Hunger and hatred reigned supreme at Auschwitz, a place of utter despair. The men lined up daily to receive a meager ration of food. Some struggled against each other to get a good place in the food line. Father Kolbe, a Catholic priest, frequently stood aside, thereby allowing others to go before him. Often he shared with others his small portion of soup or bread.

On the last day of July 1941, the camp siren at Auschwitz blared to indicate an escape. Three prisoners had miraculously vanished from their cells without a trace. The commandant was enraged. He ordered to assembly all those who lived in the same cellblocks as the escapees. He walked among them, arbitrarily choosing ten prisoners to be hauled away to the underground starvation bunker in reprisal for the escape. One of the men the commandant chose was Franciszek Gajowniczek, a married man with children. He cried out for his family. Then Father Maximillian spoke the seemingly unspeakable words, "I will take this man's place for him."

The commandant agreed to this bold proposal. Franciszek was removed from the line, and the man bearing the number 16670 burned into his flesh stepped forward and joined the other nine condemned prisoners.

The underground bunker where they were slowly starved to death had little light or air, and no food or water. Yet this place of death remained throughout the next two weeks a place of praise and prayer, especially to Mary, the selfless mother of Jesus. Father Maximilian led the group in the recitation of the rosary, in the singing of hymns, and in bolstering each other's spirits to prepare to meet God. In two weeks' time, all were dead except Maximilian. The bunker was needed for new victims to be punished by hunger, so an executioner entered the bunker and injected carbolic acid directly into a vein in Father Kolbe's left arm. Maximillian willingly gave his arm to the one ordered to kill him, a final act of surrender in an endless series of acts that embraced God's life-giving spirit.

The times in which Maximilian Kolbe lived and our own era are not all that dissimilar. Genocides in Africa and Europe in recent decades evoke memories of the atrocities unleashed by the Nazis in World War II. Times of peril are often accompanied by hunger and heroism. Perhaps the greatest danger we face as a global society is to see human privation and abject poverty as primarily economic issues, requiring only economic solutions. Rather, we are facing, as Mother Teresa suggests, a crisis within our ethos: an ethos that includes a loss of community spirit, increasing violence, and public indifference to poverty. We appear increasingly unsure about what we mean to one other. If we end up not meaning much to each other, it follows naturally that we end up neglecting our relationships with one another too.

Solidarity makes a crucial, indispensable contribution to solving the problems plaguing us in an increasingly interconnected world. Young people are often gifted with a strong instinct for perceiving the links joining us to each other. One example of this involves a number of students at the University of Maryland at College Park (UMD), who noticed that large amounts of unserved food from their school's dining halls were being discarded on a routine basis. They also had eyes to see the growing numbers of hungry people inhabiting the many shelters fewer than ten miles away in inner-city Washington, DC. The students chose to take ownership over the waste in their own school. They felt that their school's policies, their own lifestyles, and the seemingly impersonal forces that support the status quo all demanded that they act.

They put together a team of like-minded students who wanted to make a difference in our common life. In the early weeks of their efforts, students were recovering 150 to 200 pounds of food per day. They were able to donate this leftover, unserved food to shelters in the DC area, over thirty thousand meals in their first efforts in the academic year 2011–2012. They began an effort that would come to be known as the Food Recovery Network (FRN).[19] The founders of FRN, Ben Simon and Mia Zavalij, began to ask themselves, "Why doesn't every college in the United States recover food?" They researched how food is being consumed on college campuses all across the country. They discovered that approximately 75 percent to 90 percent of the United States' four thousand colleges and universities have no food recovery program.

Since its inception, the FRN has expanded to fourteen more college campuses and recovered over 120,000 pounds of food.

As a student-led initiative, FRN has been recognized as a legally incorporated nonprofit, and its student leaders are learning valuable nonprofit leadership skills. The FRN is a premier example of combining human ingenuity and innovation with the characteristically human impulse toward connection and empathy with others. The students at UMD saw not only the shameful waste in which we all are complicit but also the faces of the 43 million Americans who do not share in the food security they possess.

The founders of the FRN, Ben and Mia, have offered a simple yet stunning vision for their generation. They are set to challenge the way we live in a disposable society. It is about more than food recovery. It is about more than curbing the massive rotting of food in landfills that releases harmful methane, a potent greenhouse gas. The vision is also about investing in each other and keeping our eyes alert to the opportunity of each moment to connect to the hungry in our midst who want and deserve a place at the table and to whom we bear special responsibilities.

Ben and Mia are igniting a movement that dares to question how, collectively as a nation, we can tolerate 40 percent of the food in the United States today going uneaten. That staggering statistic is the equivalent of throwing out $165 billion worth of food each year. This loss is compounded by the massive utilization of land, water, and energy resources in agricultural production. Globally, more than two-thirds of our increasingly scarce fresh water is used in the growing of crops, much of which in the United States is never used for any good purpose. It is morally and economically unacceptable.

While the FRN may appear to be shedding a spotlight on just a single problem of food waste, the ramifications could be far-reaching if it spontaneously encourages others to question a lifestyle marked by so much waste and overconsumption. The United States, an economic and military superpower, represents a mere 5 percent of the global population. Still, we consume 24 percent of the world's energy, we collectively eat roughly 200 billion calories more than we need each day, and each of us utilizes over 100 gallons of water per day. Half the world's remaining members, on a good day, can access only 25 gallons or less.

The pervasiveness in our culture of waste and overconsumption is difficult to grasp. I sensed it only while living outside our culture. While a seminarian in Belgium, and again later as a missionary in East Africa, I discovered that the rhythms of our life are so different—conditioned, no doubt, by culture and traditions. I especially appreciated the slower pace of life experienced both in Europe and Africa compared to what I had experienced in the United States. We live frantically paced lives, and the speed is only accelerating. Many people in the United States are pathologically overextended and expect that others elsewhere are the same.

The first party I attended in Uganda was most revealing. It occasioned for me an ongoing reflection on the question, "What are the most real and valuable things in life?" While possessing little of the world's goods compared to their counterparts in wealthier regions, Africans are rich in their phenomenal spirit, and this party was one of my first experiences of it. A cake was made for the celebration. With music and dance, this cake was transported around the room, on display for all to enjoy. When it was time to eat the cake, over one hundred people shared it. This cake's size was comparable to one cake that a single family back home would have shared. Each person received a small set of crumbs; tasty for sure, but just a taste. Nothing went to waste. All enjoyed the cake; no one went without.

Slices of life such as this simple event can be wonderful sources of meditation, leading us to learn about the paradoxical, multidimensional, complex aspects of human life and behavior. Less is often more. We don't need as much as we currently consume and often waste. We can be much happier with much less. We are falsely led to believe that more is always better. The FRN presents an attractive alternative. Their recovery and subsequent sharing of food is an example of how we can set our nation on the path toward greater unity.

There is an increasing consensus, stronger than in any other era of human history, that no one's dignity should be diminished by where they were born. No person's dignity ought to be diminished by the color of his or her skin, where they are consigned to live, or the burdens of abject poverty. President Barack

Obama gave expression to this sentiment in his 2013 State of the Union message. He proclaimed,

> We also know that progress in the most impoverished parts of our world enriches us all. In many places, people live on little more than a dollar a day. So the United States will join with our allies to eradicate such extreme poverty in the next two decades: by connecting more people to the global economy and empowering women; by giving our young and brightest minds new opportunities to serve and helping communities to feed, power, and educate themselves; by saving the world's children from preventable deaths; and by realizing the promise of an AIDS-free generation.[20]

Five decades before President Obama boldly pledged to help bring about a world free from abject poverty in a relatively short time, another youthful US president challenged the nation to bring one of us to the moon and return home safely within a single decade. President Kennedy challenged us to do the seemingly impossible: set our gaze on the skies and venture farther than we had ever been. A nation was brought together around the achievement of such an audacious goal, and we succeeded. One wonders what other elusive goals could be met with imaginative leaders who direct their energies to the common good.

Notes

[1] In the wake of the earthquake in Haiti, charitable contributions were either squandered as a result of government mismanagement and corruption or misspent on costly but merely temporary relief efforts by international donors. See the BBC News report, "Haiti Quake: Why Isn't Aid Money Going to Haitians?" January 13, 2013. BBC News previously reported that the $150 billion fund intended for the reconstruction effort in Japan had been badly mismanaged ("Japan Tsumani Reconstruction Money 'Misspent,'" October 31, 2012).

[2] David Blair, "Zimbabwe: How We Aid Profligacy," *The Telegraph*, February 20, 2012.

[3] This is not to ignore the bitter racism and imposition of Jim Crow laws that prevented freed slaves from ever achieving true integration.

⁴ W. E. B. DuBois, *The Souls of Black Folks* (New York: Tribeca Books, 2013), 22.

⁵ For a compelling account of the significance of this event, read Adam Hochschild's *King Leopold's Ghost* (New York: Houghton Mifflin, 1999).

⁶ The Cynics were ancient Greek philosophers affiliated not by any formal membership in a school, but rather by a desire to live a good and noble life. Stoicism arose in ancient Greece, too, but it flourished amongst ancient Roman philosophers like Seneca, Epictetus, and Marcus Aurelius.

⁷ Many stories about Diogenes of Sinope are apocryphal. The best, though not completely reliable, source we have is Diogenes Laertius, *Lives of Eminent Philosophers* no. 184 (Loeb Classical Library, Harvard University Press, 1925), vol. 1, books 1–5.

⁸ Lee Harris, "The Cosmopolitan Illusion," *Policy Review*, April–May 2003, makes this precise argument.

⁹ Marcus Aurelius, *Meditations*, trans. Gregory Hays (New York: Modern Library, 2003).

¹⁰ Peter Singer, *One World: The Ethics of Globalization* (New Haven, CT: Yale University Press, 2002).

¹¹ Kwame Anthony Appiah, *Cosmopolitanism: Ethics in a World of Strangers* (New York: W. W. Norton, 2006).

¹² Alasdair MacIntyre, "Is Patriotism a Virtue?" *Theorizing Citizenship*, ed. Ronald Beiner (Albany, NY: SUNY Press, 1995), 209. MacIntyre is most famous for his book *After Virtue*. Here he attempts to revive the ethical thought of Aristotle and Thomas Aquinas by focusing on the need for a moral community and the articulation of a shared set of values and traditions.

¹³ This parable can be found in the Gospel of Luke (10:29–37). Or reflect on the following lines from Deuteronomy 27:19 ("Cursed be anyone who deprives the alien, the orphan, and the widow of justice") and Psalm 10:17–18 ("O LORD, you will hear the desire of the meek; you will strengthen their heart, you will incline your ear to do justice for the orphan and the oppressed, so that those from earth may strike terror no more").

¹⁴ See Immanuel Kant, *Grounding for the Metaphysics of Morals*, trans. James Ellington (Indianapolis: Hackett, 1993). Kant's ethical and political writings were inspired by the search for norms (what we ought to do) that did not rely on or presuppose any particular set of customs or beliefs about human nature. In this way, the norms could be genuinely universal in character.

¹⁵ See Kant's *Political Writings*, ed. H. S. Reiss (Cambridge: Cambridge University Press, 1991).

¹⁶ Food and Agriculture Organization of the United Nations, "Feeding the World, Eradicating Hunger: Executive Summary," World Summit on Food Security (2009).

¹⁷ Emmanuel Levinas, *Ethics and Infinity* (Pittsburgh: Duquesne University Press, 1985), 86.

[18] Leonard Foley, O.F.M., ed., *Saint of the Day: Lives and Lessons for Saints and Feasts of the New Missal* (Cincinatti: St. Anthony Messenger, 1990), 200–201.

[19] For more information about this organization, please visit www. foodrecoverynetwork.org.

[20] US president Barack Obama, State of the Union Address, February 13, 2013, as quoted by Leslie Pitterson, "International Development and Obama's State of the Union Address," *U.S. News and World Report*, February 13, 2013.

Chapter 2

The Power of Moral Argument

> The third-rate mind is only happy when it is thinking
> with the majority. The second-rate mind is only happy
> when it is thinking with the minority. The first-rate
> mind is only happy when it is thinking.
>
> —*A. A. Milne*[1]

Jim

In his masterwork, *Republic*, Plato recounts a story that has
come to be known as "the myth of the metals."[2] The story is
designed to promote patriotic values and to determine, once and
for all, who should rule. In the story, citizens are told that each of
them has a certain kind of metal mixed into his soul. The kind of
metal (i.e., gold, silver, bronze, and iron) in one's soul determines
one's role in society. Not surprisingly, those with bronze or iron
in their souls could not legitimately claim the authority to rule.
Most of the time, the metal in one's soul would be passed down
to the next generation, although there could be exceptional cases
of a gold soul coming from a union of bronze souls. Nonetheless,
this myth could help promote a rigid social hierarchy that would
avoid any complicated questions about the legitimacy of those in
power. It could help reconcile those with inferior souls to their
position in society, while supplying those reluctant to rule with
a natural basis for fulfilling their duty.

The notion that the metallic qualities of one's soul could be
used as a standard to justify inequality is not as absurd as it may

seem. There is no significant difference between Plato's myth of the metals and the idea that one's blood makes one more or less noble. What we might call the "myth of blood" has been used to support the divine right of kings, the natural nobility of the aristocracy, and the rigid caste system that designates some human beings as untouchable. It motivated a frenetic pseudoscientific search in the nineteenth century for a biological confirmation of racial differences. It has even served as the philosophical justification for genocide. And despite the prevalence of the idea of natural equality, this blood myth persists in various forms, even covertly in instances of casual racism and simple-minded bigotry.

If metal and blood are the stuff of myth, then perhaps an enlightened people can rationally discover and argue for the truth of equality among all people. Some Christians have promoted this idea, accepting that each individual is created in the image and likeness of God, as confirmed by secular Enlightenment philosophers who defended each individual's equal access to the "natural light of reason."[3] Although the idea of cosmopolitanism has its origin in ancient Greek and Roman philosophy, it was not yet fully developed at the time. Living according to nature rather than custom marks a step toward breaking down the fundamental differences between individuals, but this idea alone does not provide specific moral obligations to those outside of one's community. Even the meaning of the concept of equality changed, from the ancient Greek democratic notion of "equality amongst equals"[4] to the Christian and Enlightenment claim that all individuals are, in fact, equal.[5] The expansion of the category of those who are equal brought with it an expansion of political and moral rights and duties. Sacred and secular agreement on this issue makes the idea far stronger than it would have been otherwise.

Is it possible, then, to *argue* for the cosmopolitan ideal? Some recent attempts have gained much attention, either for their impeccable logic or for the fact that, although clever, they ring hollow. The most interesting case is the one in which both conditions are true—a beautiful argument that is ultimately unpersuasive. Peter Singer, a public philosopher and professor at Princeton, often prompts just this reaction in his readers. He published a provocative editorial in September 1999 that is still hotly debated.[6] In the article, Singer indulges in a thought experiment concerning a man named Bob who could save a child in danger of being hit by a runaway train. All he has to do is flip the switch to move the train to an adjoining track. By diverting the direction of the train, however, he would destroy his precious Bugatti, parked precariously on the other track. Bob chooses not to flip the switch, and Singer assumes that most readers would judge him harshly for this decision.

Although the example is far-fetched—who parks a Bugatti on a train track?—the message is clear. Material things, however valuable, cannot match the truly precious character of human life. The difference is so great that it does not even make sense to weigh the two against each other. And yet, says Singer, we are all in Bob's position, every hour of the day. We, too, could save a child's life simply by donating the money that we spend frivolously on material things. Singer anticipates the obvious objections to this view, especially the claim that we have no guarantee that the money will actually be used to help those in need. Citing US philosopher Peter Unger, Singer insists that even $200 can make a decisive contribution to saving the life of a child.[7] That number takes into account all the overhead expenses and bureaucratic wrangling that accompanies foreign aid efforts.

When my students read Singer's editorial, they often credit him with devising a compelling argument, even if they also criticize the details of his example. But they find themselves compelled to agree with Singer only in a *logical* sense, not in the *practical* sense that truly matters. In other words, they agree that his argument for cosmopolitanism is rationally sound while doubting whether it would actually motivate a change in behavior. Echoing Unger, Singer even includes the phone numbers for Oxfam and UNICEF just in case his readers find his view practically compelling. Most readers never seem to make the call.

How can an idea so logically convincing be so practically inert? Perhaps this is a problem for moral argument as such: being intellectually convinced and having my heart moved enough to change my behavior are quite different things. A world of difference resides between the obligations I have to those I love, or have at least met, and the obligations I have to those whose suffering I do not witness. At the very least, one kind of obligation often requires no argument, as it is rooted in the deep bonds between loved ones, while the other does. And if we begin with the obligations that seem natural and obvious, a huge leap in imagination seems necessary to expand those same obligations to those whose suffering is unseen. Perhaps Alasdair MacIntyre's argument from the previous chapter was right. Maybe our moral obligations cannot be conceived rationally outside of the bonds of community, custom, and tradition.

An easy conclusion would be that we are moral hypocrites who fail to practice what we preach. But anyone who actually cares about motivating a change in behavior would do well to respect this disparity and to search for ways of bridging the gap. Immediately after rejecting the plausibility of Singer's account, many of my students make an effort to explain why they did not pick up the phone to donate. This explanation is often done either in an apologetic tone or in a tone that suggests that they are not actually in the same position as Bob. I remind them that their excuses are unnecessary if the idea is truly implausible. Why, then, do they insist on giving an account of something that does not seem to require explanation?

The intuition to defend oneself in this case might be explained by better understanding what it means to be complicit with injustice. Maybe my students are not like Bob, at least in the sense that they did not directly cause the death of a child. But moral responsibility makes this discussion of *causing* a death much more complicated. If we can accept the intellectual plausibility of Singer's scenario, then we might also be upset with the cognitive dissonance between action and belief. Seeing that our donation could play a decisive role in saving a life is not much of a leap. Nor is it a stretch to acknowledge that our inaction allows such injustice to persist.

A classic statement of complicity appears in Martin Luther King Jr.'s "Letter from a Birmingham Jail."[8] King focuses his criticism not on those who directly commit injustice but rather on those "moderates" who recognize that injustice is wrong but allow it to happen through their own inaction. Consider the difference between the predominantly white clergy (King's target audience) and the Ku Klux Klan. There was no real mystery to the Klan: the organization might have been secretive in some ways, but their politics and policies were clear and viciously expressed in public. So why does King reserve his most forceful criticism for the clergy? He expresses his disappointment that they have abandoned their divine purpose: to be "thermostats"[9] and not merely "thermometers" in a broken society. They are divinely missioned to be "creative extremists" like Christ, agents for social change rather than passive observers of society. In a nonintuitive way, the clergy was responsible for the crimes committed in the South, because they recognized the injustice and did not do anything. To see and not act is worse, from the standpoint of moral responsibility, than to be an ignorant member of a lynch mob. If moral responsibility is at all related to the recognition of injustice, intellectual conviction and practical conviction are inextricably connected.

Numerous literary, philosophical, and biblical sources confirm this observation. For instance, Revelation 3:16 states, "So, because you are lukewarm, and neither hot nor cold, I will spit you out of my mouth." An ignorant man who commits evil acts could, in principle, have his heart transformed. He could, over time, be brought to see the world differently. Take, for instance, Libby Phelps Alvarez, a defector from the infamous Westboro Baptist Church. This supposed church specializes in antihomosexual hate speech, focusing most of its energy on picketing. Westboro especially prefers to picket the funerals of dead US soldiers, claiming that God is punishing the United States for its cultural decline. Libby thought that she was doing God's work, but over time she came to realize that she was in a cult. She summoned the strength to leave. Now imagine that she knew the whole time that participating in such an organization was morally wrong. Let's assume that, despite this knowledge, she continued to attend the events or worked behind the scenes in some fashion. If her unwillingness to leave is the result of lukewarm moral character, and not simply ignorance or fear, then what could possibly set her on the right path? If her participation was clearheaded and freely chosen, then doesn't she deserve more moral blame? These lukewarm souls can also be found in the vestibule of Dante's Inferno, forever running in circles, chasing a whirling banner, not fit to be damned:

> This miserable state is borne by the wretched souls of those who lived without disgrace yet without praise. They intermingle with that wicked band of angels, not rebellious and not faithful to God, who held themselves apart. Loath to impair its beauty, Heaven casts them out, and depth of Hell does not receive them lest on their account the evil angels gloat.[10]

John Milton expressed a related sentiment in 1644: "I cannot praise a fugitive and cloistered virtue unexercised and unbreathed, that never sallies out and sees her adversary, but slinks out of the race, where that immortal garland is to be run for, not without dust and heat. Assuredly we bring not innocence into the world; we bring impurity much rather; that which purifies us is trial, and trial is by what is contrary."[11]

A more contemporary reference comes in Theodore Roosevelt's 1910 "Citizenship in a Republic" speech at the Sorbonne, where he famously praised the "man in the arena" and mocked "those cold and timid souls who neither know victory nor defeat."[12] Roosevelt calls this man "the critic," who self-assuredly observes rather than acts, fearful of taking a risk and making a bad decision. On the contrary, "the man in the arena" fully commits himself. He risks losing, but he also has much to gain if he strives for what is right and succeeds. He is not afraid to stand up for what he believes is right, unwilling to embrace the cold comfort of clean hands.

The shared insight of these references is their disdain for those who abdicate moral responsibility for taking action, preferring instead to remain on the sidelines unscathed. The idea of complicity reveals this attitude to be a false form of moral perfection, since it mistakenly assumes that one's hands are clean as long as one avoids the direct infliction of harm. Yet harm can also be inflicted indirectly, and the actions of those who recognize harm as unjust can prevent it.

Another example of this is US foreign policy just before World War II. Many isolationists cautioned that we should stay out of foreign entanglements. Some of the reasons offered were strictly pragmatic: it would be too risky militarily to become involved in another war sparked in Europe. Other reasons purported to be morally righteous. Wouldn't it be better to stay out of conflict and avoid the inevitable deaths? While hindsight affords us a crystal-clear perspective on this debate, we can still ask whether the concern over inflicting harm is often just a way to rationalize our own prudent inaction.

The moral difference between the direct and indirect infliction of harm during wartime is an ancient distinction in Catholic ethics. St. Augustine and St. Thomas Aquinas both formulated ethical principles that have been incorporated into what today is known as just war theory.[13] The principles of just war license some "collateral damage," the deaths inevitably but indirectly caused by war. For instance, while targeting a hospital would be unjust and immoral, it is not, in principle, immoral to cause indirectly the death of someone who happens to be standing near a high-value target. If the decision was made out of an abundance of caution, and as long as such incidental damage is limited and proportional, it is not morally prohibited. Critics of this idea might point out that any loss of life is unethical. Still, in a complicated world, the perfect is often the enemy of the good.

In early June 1944, deep into the all-encompassing conflict of World War II, General Dwight Eisenhower agonized over the decision to invade Normandy, France. The dangerous mission was a crucial part of the plan to overthrow Adolf Hitler and his advancing army. Eisenhower knew that such an invasion would risk the lives of many thousands of his troops. He even looked a few of these men in the eye before the attack, having toured the bases to gauge the morale of the soldiers. But he also knew that the purpose of the attack—liberating France and stopping the spread of Nazism throughout Europe—represented a superior moral goal. Achieving that goal without sacrifice would not be possible.

If we were so risk averse as to avoid all possible negative consequences, we would be incapable of making any decision at all. But this inaction, this failure to act, often leads to an even more violent and unjust state of affairs. If Eisenhower had acted like the critic rather than the man in the arena, would the outcome of the war have changed? On the other hand, if the Normandy invasion had turned into a brutal massacre of forces, which it might have been were it not for some tremendous luck and clever counterintelligence, would Eisenhower's risk have marked him as a murderer? Would that judgment have been deserved?

We return to the question of the cosmopolitan ideal. As we have seen, intellectual conviction and practical conviction are quite different. The idea of complicity shows how deeply connected they are, but the sad truth is that even this idea often lacks motivational force—especially in the case of suffering that remains unseen. If King's exhortation to the moderates in Birmingham was effective, a possible explanation would be that they lived among the people who were being so badly mistreated. The famous bus boycotts in Montgomery demonstrated to some reticent individuals that serious social and economic consequences would result for their continued discrimination. The famous maxim, "Injustice anywhere is a threat to justice everywhere," is likely more convincing if the injustice is taking place next door instead of half a world away.

If this is so, then saying that moral argument alone cannot be relied upon to be practically convincing seems right. The very quality that makes it so appealing—its impersonal, unbiased character—arguably undermines its motivational force. Moral argument permits the cold and timid souls to operate with their flawed notions of moral perfection, since the logic of the argument at no point implicates me or any other individual personally. The conclusion it forces me to accept intellectually is that something should be done about the bizarre tradeoffs we make between material luxuries and human life. It does not follow logically that I am the one responsible for doing it. In other words, most people would likely be convinced by the idea that the poor should not starve. They would identify a hypothetical world where everyone had enough food and water as being morally superior to our present world. Yet this argument is not enough to convince them that they are personally responsible for helping to make this hypothetical world real.

A related difficulty with moral argument arises when one considers the relative value of our material goods. At first it might seem daunting to comprehend giving enough money to save a life. All sorts of ready-made excuses naturally follow, such as "If I had more money, I would give more," and "Why should I accept this burden when more capable people fail to do their part?" But when one learns how little is actually required to make a difference, a different set of excuses arise: "That much cannot possibly make a difference," and "If that is all it takes, then surely lots of other people already contribute."

Either the amount is perceived to be too great (in which case it is simply unaffordable) or too insignificant to bother. When a commercial claims that for the cost of a cup of coffee a day you can save a life, it might ironically dissuade one from contributing. Psychologists call this the "bystander effect," which holds that people are less likely to intervene in cases of distress and emergency when they perceive a greater number of witnesses. Instead of sharing responsibility, everyone assumes that someone else will get involved. Responsibility becomes diffuse—spread over the total number of witnesses—rather than perceived as individual and even as personal. In this case, you are never really forced into making a moral decision (since the amount is deemed insignificant), despite the fact that the value of your contribution is exponentially greater once it reaches its destination. Any argument that fails to recognize the relative value of the contribution at stake misunderstands the mind-set of the potential donor.

The bystander effect has been studied in ingenious ways. For instance, Bibb Latané and John Darley designed a series of experiments to measure the relationship between the number of witnesses during an emergency and the reaction time of those involved.[14] They determined not only that individual participants were less likely to intervene when there were multiple witnesses but also that they reported no change in their own behavior. This outcome suggests that we fail to recognize our own obligation to act *and* that we are unaware of our self-deception. Imagine if the conditions of the experiment were extrapolated to include everyone capable of contributing to feed the hungry. If responsibility becomes more diffuse as the group gets larger, is it any wonder that so few of us act based on argument alone?

A final concern with the power of moral argument concerns its relationship with our deeply held beliefs. Richard Posner, a prominent judge and public intellectual, takes issue with Singer's assumption that ethical argument should trump what Posner calls our "moral instincts."[15] For Singer, every boundary between human beings is, in a deep sense, artificial. Geography, for instance, is not a morally relevant fact, and proximity to suffering should not determine the degree of our moral obligation. Yet Posner claims that human beings are essentially pack animals that defend their own kind. The mistake of the cosmopolitan is to assume that the bonds of the family, the community, and even the country can be indefinitely expanded.

If I define myself in terms of these local and specific obligations, then does that simply make me prejudiced, or does it reveal a powerful moral instinct that argument cannot refute? And, as Posner points out in his fascinating debate with Singer, doesn't the cosmopolitan make the opposite assumption? What makes the assumption of equality between individuals more *rational* than a defense of the deep intuition that our obligations are not equal? How is the idea that proximity to suffering is morally irrelevant any more self-evident than the claim that proximity is morally crucial? Saying that it is more intellectually convincing is not enough, since, as we have already seen, this point is not sufficient from a practical perspective. If both of these views rely upon presuppositions, then perhaps the cosmopolitan attempt to replace myth—whether it concerns metal or blood—with rational argument is itself an attempt at mythmaking. Singer might think that his myth is morally superior, but those who disseminated the myth of the metals and the myth of blood surely thought so, too. When we affirm an argument as being the only rational solution, we disregard everything else as an irrational myth and thereby undermine powerful sources of motivation. If the bystander effect teaches us something about human nature, then perhaps those who defend local, small-scale obligations are the ones who properly understand the psychological roots of responsibility. And might it not be more rational, at least in some sense, to prefer to help those in my community and even my country, since I regard their fate as more closely bound to my own? If kinship, custom, tradition, intuition, and even human emotion are cast aside as irrational imposters and sources of bias, then we are left with the natural light of reason. But what is left for that light to illuminate, and how can we live by its conclusions alone? If claiming that moral argument provides a rational antidote to the irrationality of myth seems insufficient and even deceptive, then something else is required to make the cosmopolitan ideal real.

To return briefly to the quote from A. A. Milne that introduced this chapter, something else must help us to develop from third-rate and second-rate thinkers (satisfied with following the majority or minority, respectively) in to first-rate thinkers. Perhaps what distinguishes first-rate thinking is the way it brings together intellectual and practical conviction. Lesser thinkers seize upon some idea that they profess to be true without examining the underlying reasons. Deficient thinking does not produce reliable actions, since it amounts to passively (rather than personally) accepting what the majority or minority claims. In the next chapter, we look at one possible solution to the problem of genuinely thinking about cosmopolitanism: appealing to the heart and not just the head (supplementing *intellectually* convincing arguments with *practically* convincing calls for empathy).

Don

Almost immediately after his birth, Jesus and his parents became refugees. They fled their homeland, a place of great danger, journeying to Egypt, the faraway place, in the hopes of escaping a powerful king bent on unleashing deadly violence upon them. Two millennia later, this same story is still being played out in our day with millions of refugees across the globe.

In 2005 I found myself working in Uganda. At that time, civil strife had turned the whole of northern Uganda into a chaotic war zone. The entire population lived in fear of marauding rebels. Since the government had imposed strict requirements that whole regions of innocent civilians in northern Uganda needed to be restricted to internally displaced persons (IDP) camps, no one could farm. Food supplies from the UN World Food Program were scarce. In the summer of 2005 I visited an IDP camp in northern Uganda with a group of humanitarian outreach workers. The impression that overtook me immediately was a sense that this could be the most exceedingly cramped and overcrowded place on our planet. Everywhere I looked I saw a vast sea of humanity. The first hut I entered housed a multigenerational family of ten persons in a single room. In full display everywhere in the camp were two conflicting realities: staggering numbers of people (over twenty-five thousand children, women, and men) coupled with a scarcity of everything people need to live. There was a severe scarcity of water, little food, not enough firewood for fuel; medicine was lacking, and it seemed to me that people were literally living on hope.

One elderly grandmother, upon learning that I was a priest, asked me if I would please bless something for her. I was happy to oblige, and she took me on a long walk into the heart of the IDP camp. I presumed she wanted me to bless a religious article like a rosary or medal. I was wrong. She took me to the grave of her thirty-year-old daughter, a mother of four small children, who had succumbed to suicide the previous month. This young mother just couldn't bear to see her children go hungry, and she felt absolutely defeated by her circumstances. We stood there together at her grave asking God to heal and comfort and feed this family.

The violence of war breeds hunger and privation like nothing else. Routinely, whenever the world has been at war, civilian populations have died in large, often incalculable numbers. Last night an estimated 43 million persons or more could not sleep at home because their home is no longer a safe place to dwell.[16] They are reduced by a civil strife beyond their control to live as nomads against their will. The rest of the world calls them by two names: refugees or internally displaced persons. Refugees are those who have fled across their national borders into another nation because of the imminent danger of violence. IDPs have been forced to flee their home region but have not crossed the border into another nation. They cannot farm their homelands, engage in their normal income-generating projects, raise their families, or even feel safe and secure. They are strangers in their own homeland, and the disorientation they must feel makes them internally displaced within themselves as well.

Unquestionably, their greatest enemies are scheming despots bent on one thing: the ruthless and unrelenting pursuit of their own power. Refugees appear to despots as little more than pawns to be used, manipulated, and even killed in pursuit of their ever tightening grip on power. Despotic regimes have engaged in deliberate strategies of displacing persons, preventing the delivery of relief supplies. Rulers have used scorched-earth policies aimed at destroying livestock and food supplies, slowly allowing massive civilian populations to suffer hunger unto death.

In the final years of the twentieth century, the country then known as Yugoslavia was breaking apart in the worst and most violent ways imaginable. In war's most barbaric expressions, both hunger and rape become weapons in the arsenal of those bent on destroying a nation and its people. The regime of Yugoslav president Slobodan Milosevic set in motion a strategy resulting in countless Albanians being trapped inside Kosovo, freezing and starving. The world, from a safe distance, watched their slow deaths. They died in the heart of Europe, unable to get enough food and basic necessities to stay alive. President Clinton attempted to put a human face on this faraway war by telling gripping narratives of reports he had received of the ethnic cleansing being conducted in a way reminiscent of Hitler's holocaust in World War II. Clinton noted how "Serb forces, their faces often concealed by masks, as they were before in Bosnia, have rounded up Kosovar women and repeatedly raped them. They have said to children: Go into the woods and die of hunger."[17]

A despotic leader who has used hunger as a weapon of war in its most brutalizing way is the Sudanese president Omar el-Bashir.[18] Sudan is a massive country, the largest in all of Africa and the tenth-largest country in the world based on area. It is also a land of sorrow. It has experienced the most protracted period of civil war of any nation in the past century, enduring across thirty-nine years, 1955–1972 and 1983–2005. Roughly 2 million people have died in its aftermath, largely from the resulting famine and disease. Four million people in southern Sudan have been displaced, some finding a new life outside and far from their homeland. The people of south Sudan have been forced, for decades, to fight to protect their way of life, their faith, their natural resources, and their very lives from dominating forces in the central Arabic government in Khartoum. A generation of Sudanese can remember only bloodshed and destruction since their early childhood.

The camps in Darfur, in western Sudan, have been described by eyewitness accounts as resembling Auschwitz. Omar el-Bashir is the first sitting head of state for whom an arrest warrant has been issued by the International Criminal Court (ICC) in The Hague. The indictment includes charges of crimes against humanity, murder, extermination, forcible transfer, torture, and rape. There is evidence of Omar el-Bashir's personally directing attacks on the civilian population and pillaging. Pillaging leaves refugees without anything: including food, water, medicine, and hope.

When it was announced that the ICC had charged President el-Bashir, his first reaction was so telling. He immediately expelled thirteen humanitarian aid agencies from the Darfur region, causing suffering to escalate. It was a show of power: the power of one man's decision to wreak havoc and hunger on the many. In the protracted civil war between the Arab-controlled Sudanese government in the north and the black, principally Christian, Sudanese in the south, the weapon most often unleashed on the southern Sudanese was hunger: their villages pillaged by marauders, their cattle hauled off, their way of life destroyed. So often the people who have fought epic battles in our time just for the right to survive remain at a distance from us. We admire their resilience and courage from afar, but we have no personal experience of them and their ordeals. Indeed, it has been said that we live in a world of people whose faces we never meet. However, the case of the young Sudanese who have endured the longest civil war of our lifetimes has changed this perspective. The world has come to know them as the "Lost Boys of Sudan."[19] At one point in time they numbered as many as twenty thousand boys of the Dinka and Nuer tribes who fled their homes when their villages were attacked by militias from the north. Many of them were tending to their family's herds outside the villages when the attacks began, and they simply hid in the bush to escape the attacks. They fled en masse, traveling on foot for years in a biblical-like wandering in the Sahara desert, searching for safe refuge. Over half of them would die on their journey to an uncertain future. Predictably, the principal causes of their deaths were starvation and dehydration. Desperate for fluids in the burning desert, some of the boys carried their own urine with them wherever they went.

Between November 2000 and September 2001, approximately thirty-eight hundred Sudanese children and young adults, predominantly boys and young men, were resettled in the United States. They became our neighbors. They entrusted their stories to us. I have befriended the Sudanese young adult community that arrived in Cleveland in 2001 and been inspired by their capacity to believe still in the power of goodness over all else. These young people have had the world at its worst thrown at them: the sudden loss of parental nurture and guidance; the denial of secure access to food, water, and medicine; and being forced to fight daily just for survival.

With thousands of boys his own age, Majok Madut fled his home in southern Sudan while he was still a child. He left behind everyone he loved and the way of life he cherished. Many of his friends died as they fled violence in their homeland. They died unable to protect themselves from wild animals, the bullets of hostile governments, and the deadly heat and thirst of the Sahara. Majok possessed nothing for protection except the brotherhood he forged with those in his company who were plunged into the same fate. That brotherhood literally kept him alive amid endless rounds of peril.

After years of wandering in search of safety, Majok and his companions were finally settled at a sprawling UN refugee camp at Kakuma, in northern Kenya, where he lived for the next nine years. Upward of eighty thousand people were cramped into a desolate location designed to house less than half that number of persons. UN officials reluctantly had to place Kakuma residents on half rations as food supplies continued to dwindle and donations to its UN World Food Program declined. Most Kakuma residents often ate only once a day. Hunger pangs forced some to leave the camp in search of wild edibles, roots, berries, anything to supplement the meager provisions that were distributed twice a month.

In childhood, Majok contracted rickets. The primary cause of rickets is a vitamin D deficiency. The majority of people suffering from rickets are children afflicted with severe malnutrition. In his teenage years Majok began to suffer from a partial paralysis in both legs. He spent enormous energy trying to overcome the limitations this brought on to him. He walked with a limp, often needing crutches, but it made him all the more determined to walk and to walk all the faster. In the camp Majok was the consummate street vendor. He'd hustle, selling plastic mats for people to sleep on, wheat flour, and oil for cooking. He liked to care for himself; he was by nature fiercely independent. When he eventually resettled in the United States, he would come to call Cleveland home. He was one of the nearly four thousand young Sudanese who were accepted for permanent entry. Clearly the Sudanese government did not want them ever to return, assuming they would be hostile toward a government that they believed had unleashed deadly and unwarranted violence upon their villages and families.

Their journey to a new homeland was not easy. Names were posted on billboards at Kakuma of those chosen for resettlement in the United States. Those who saw their own names posted knew immediately that their lives would be changed forever in ways they could not anticipate. A distance of more than eight thousand miles separates the Sudan from the United States. Many of my Sudanese friends were thrilled to have greater personal security as well as greater financial and food security. At the same time they longed for the familiar faces and places of their childhood.

Discovering new ways of living is always challenging. That adventure of discovery began while they were still in flight toward their uncertain future. As the airline steward approached with meals, some feared saying yes to the supper, because they had no money in their pockets. When assured that the cost of the meal was already included in their airline ticket, they were still reluctant to eat. Nothing they had ever eaten before looked like this meal, and everything appeared strange and unappealing. One of the leaders of the group stood and walked up and down the aisle of the airplane. Seeing the other passengers enjoying their meal, he sat down and told himself, *They are human and they are eating this meal. I am human, too. I will follow their example.*

Because of his limited mobility, Majok had difficulty finding work. After two years trying to get a job, he was offered work by the Cleveland Clinic at one of their upscale restaurants as a short-order cook. He was thrilled. He arrived daily for work at least an hour early to show his appreciation for this opportunity. When he was told by new friends in the United States that he could go on disability and receive his needed financial resources from the government, he couldn't believe it. He wouldn't accept it. His moral instinct wouldn't allow him to take from the commonweal without first contributing to it.

Two weeks before Christmas in 2006, an unknown assailant shot and killed Majok in a drive-by shooting on the streets of Cleveland. Police believe it was likely a gang initiation. He was waiting on a street corner for the bus to take him home after work. His wallet and cell phone and other valuables were not stolen. Majok had managed to stay alive in a violent war zone that had witnessed over 2 million deaths in his lifetime, escaping to the safety he believed he had long last found in the United

States. His physical therapist told me that when she met Majok in 2001 he did not speak English very well, but he was able to communicate through his heart—in the universal language of love. Majok had no enemies. It happened that someone who never knew him, who could never have realized all the death-defying ordeals he was forced to endure, simply ended his life on a whim, killing him randomly.

The tragic circumstances of Majok's untimely death remind us not only how precious and unpredictable life is but also how interconnected we have become. The question of whether the United States should intervene in the ongoing crisis in the Sudan has been painfully unresolved. More often than not, the topic is simply ignored. Yet, in the case of Majok and his fellow Lost Boys brothers, we have many examples of victims of violence who have worked diligently to become members of our local community. When Majok was brutally murdered, we lost one of our own.

Rabbi Abraham Joshua Heschel, the renowned Jewish theologian, often taught his rabbinic students that the whole of Scripture could be synthesized in a single word: Remember. Without memory of what God has done for us there is no faith and no hope; there can be no embrace of the future. My Sudanese friends have the greatest capacity for remembrance of any set of people I've ever encountered. Even though they were very young at the time, they can detail for us with great specificity their days spent as child nomads in the Sahara desert. They recall vividly what their unmet longing for food and water felt like for them. They remember eating dried-up leaves off dying trees because, as they scavenged for food, they found nothing else edible. The memory of the constant strain of parched throats has never faded. They can never forget the generosity of those who, with little water, were willing to share with them when they had no water at all. Above all else, they hold in sacred memory how their shared suffering brought them closer to each other in one of our world's truly remarkable brotherhoods. In that remembrance, Isaac's Wells was born.

Isaac Dahl, one of the twenty-nine Sudanese young men who settled in Cleveland in 2001, returned home in 2006 to his

village of Duluit Bol in southern Sudan on his first visit back
since fleeing his war-torn homeland. His most powerful remembrance from that reunion with loved ones was witnessing their
struggle to secure access to clean water. In his new home in a
neighborhood of Cleveland's Westside, the water flows without
fail whenever he turns on the faucet. Isaac's appreciation of the
food and water security that he and his wife and children now
enjoy is incomparable in my experience. Isaac is one of the most
grateful and happy persons I have ever known. Remembering his
thirst in the desert, and having never forgotten the people he left
behind in southern Sudan, Isaac wanted to become a catalyst for
others to know the same blessings he has received.

Together with his friend and mentor Sister Mary Frances
Harrington, Isaac gathered together the Sudanese young adult
community with a sizable contingent of their Cleveland friends.
In November 2000 Sister Mary Frances had heard of these
young Sudanese before they ever arrived in the United States.
She worshiped at St. Agnes–Our Lady of Fatima Parish in the
heart of Cleveland. From the pulpit she heard of the needs of
the forty refugees soon to arrive in their neighborhood from
the southern part of Sudan. Sister Mary Frances had worked for
three years with Bosnian refugees arriving in Cleveland, and she
was concerned that these Sudanese refugees would bear even
deeper marks of pain.

Isaac, Sister Mary Frances, and their neighbors and friends
forged a common goal: to build wells in each of the fifteen villages in southern Sudan that these young men were forced to leave.
As a result of their efforts, Isaac's Wells was born. This organization
reaches out directly from Cleveland to the Sudan, relying on the
generosity and determination of Sudanese and US citizens alike.
Together they seek a more united world enjoying water security.
While many of the Sudanese already send home to their families
in Africa whatever resources they have accrued, they feel driven
to offer even more in pursuit of water security for those they
were forced to leave behind when they fled the war.

The Cleveland Lost Boys of Sudan have been invited to make
presentations in schools, community centers, youth groups, and

countless churches all throughout northeast Ohio. Listening to their stories is simultaneously captivating and painful. Many of them speak in a soft tone of voice, requiring listeners to lean in close so as not to miss a single word of an enthralling message. I presumed that it must be devastating for these young men to invoke once again the details of their horrific ordeals. Just the opposite appears to be the case. These young men love to tell their stories. They find it liberating and healing for them to reveal what has been held in their memory for so long. When they return to a high school, the students often greet them enthusiastically. The high school students often accord the Lost Boys near rock-star status, admiring the resilience they brought to the struggle.

After hearing these young men talk, teens sometimes come forward to share an especially painful experience of their own. Jackie Tuckerman, a mentor who arranges all their presentations, has commented, "I have been brought to tears watching them comfort some of these kids. I have marveled at the compassion and patience they have, given the level of violence and injustice they have experienced."

The writer Barbara Hardy has written that "we dream in narrative, daydream in narrative, remember, anticipate, hope, despair, believe, doubt, plan, revise, criticize, construct, gossip, learn, hate, and love by narrative."[20] I see my Sudanese friends building up hope for a more humane world, story by story. They do so in their uncanny ability to capture the imaginations and hearts of those whose experiences of life are drastically different from their own. They invite their listeners into solidarity with those still yearning for the gift of clean, fresh water. The answer is always yes.

Solidarity emerges as funds are donated by the various audiences who hear the stories and take action. One by one, Isaac's Wells has been sending the Cleveland Sudanese young adults back home to their villages in what is in 2013 the newest independent nation on earth—the Republic of South Sudan. They meet with the elders in their home villages to assess the needs. How many wells are needed? Where is the best location to place them? They also meet with the well-digging company and offer a watchful presence, representing the interests of the donors who want this project to succeed on time and on budget.

The true blessing here is that each of these young men, absent from their families and communities for more than two decades, are returning at long last to their home village, bearing a much sought-after treasure: water in steady supply. The new nation of South Sudan has overwhelming needs, but clean water is at the top of the long list. The villagers have a concrete assurance that their sons, lost to war, never lost their love and affection for family and homeland.

Notes

[1] A. A. Milne, "War with Honour," *Macmillan War Pamphlets*, Issue 2 (1940).

[2] See Plato, *Republic*, in *Collected Works of Plato*, trans. John Cooper (Indianapolis: Hackett, 1997), 414c–415e.

[3] In the seventeenth and eighteenth centuries, philosophers of the Enlightenment tried to provide rational foundations for beliefs that did not rely on custom and tradition. Their methods were secular and universal, even if their personal beliefs and philosophical goals were at times religious. Relying on the natural light of reason, they promoted a method that could, in principle, be carried out by whoever was careful enough to think in an unbiased way. For a good example of this approach, see René Descartes, *Discourse on Method and Meditations on First Philosophy*, 4th ed., trans. Donald Cress (Indianapolis: Hackett, 1999).

[4] To investigate a wide variety of primary sources dealing with the concepts of citizenship and equality in ancient Greece, see the definitive collection, *Ancient Greek Democracy: Readings and Sources*, ed. Eric W. Robinson (Oxford: Blackwell, 2004).

[5] This is not to deny that the expansion of the concept of equality was precarious and uncertain. Take, for instance, the fight for equality in the United States, a country whose founding documents profess the equality of all.

[6] Peter Singer, "The Singer Solution to World Poverty," *New York Times*, September 5, 1999.

[7] Peter Unger, *Living High and Letting Die: Our Illusion of Innocence* (New York: Oxford University Press, 1996), 148.

[8] Martin Luther King Jr., "Letter from a Birmingham Jail," in *I Have a Dream: Writings and Speeches That Changed the World* (New York: HarperOne, 2003), 83–101.

[9] Ibid.

[10] Dante Alighieri, *The Inferno*, trans. Robert Hollander and Jean Hollander (New York: Doubleday, 2000), 3:34–69.

[11] John Milton, *Areopagitica* (H. Regnery Co., 1949).

[12] Theodore Roosevelt, "The Man in the Arena," speech at the Sorbonne, April 23, 1910, http://www.theodore-roosevelt.com.

[13] For a thorough and contemporary discussion of these principles, see Michael Walzer, *Just and Unjust Wars: A Moral Argument with Historical Illustrations* (New York: Basic Books, 1977).

[14] Bibb Latane and John Darley, "Bystander 'Apathy,'" *American Scientist* 57 (1969): 244–68.

[15] See the intriguing debate between Singer and Posner: "Animal Rights," *Slate Magazine*, June 12, 2001.

[16] Simon Rogers, "UNHCR 2011 Refugee Statistics: Full Data," *The Guardian*, June 20, 2011.

[17] President Bill Clinton, *U.S. Congressional Record, Proceedings and Debates of the 106th Congress*, 1st session, vol. 145, part 7, May 13, 1999, p. 9504.

[18] See John C. Bradshaw, "The Case against Sudanese President Omar al Bashir," *The Hill*, April 5, 2013.

[19] See Karen Long, "Coming to America," *Plain Dealer Sunday Magazine*, September 30, 2001.

[20] Barbara Hardy, "Towards a Poetics of Fiction: An Approach through Narrative," *Novel: A Forum on Fiction* 2, no. 1 (Autumn 1968): 5–14.

Chapter 3

Appeals to Emotion
It's the Heart, Not the Head!

We think we understand the rules when we become adults, but what we really experience is a narrowing of the imagination.

—*David Lynch*

Jim

In late February 2012 a video produced by the activist group Invisible Children called *Kony 2012* became an Internet sensation. In a matter of weeks, it received tens of millions of hits on YouTube. On its Twitter account, the group made an explicitly cosmopolitan appeal for its cause, claiming, "Where you live shouldn't determine whether you live." Jason Russell, a cofounder of the group, makes a promise to a young Ugandan boy who watched his brother slaughtered that he would do everything in his power to stop Joseph Kony, the brutal leader of the Lord's Resistance Army. Russell also attempts to explain the situation to his own young son, who encourages his father to "stop the bad guys from being mean." In return for a small donation, converts to cosmopolitanism would receive a bracelet they could wear as a public sign of their support.

Criticism of the group and its video message was fast and furious. Some critics questioned the practices of the charity. Others reminded us of the complexity of any geopolitical problem, even one that seems as straightforward as this one. But two intriguing and related complaints stood out: the idea that the video promoted what has come to be known as "slacktivism": a form of "low-effort, feel-good activism among millions of college students and young people mesmerized by the video that does very little to help anyone on the ground in Central Africa."[1] The second interesting complaint comes from the same article. The author quotes a Nigerian-born author named Teju Cole, who provocatively writes, "The White Savior Industrial Complex is not about justice. It is about having a big emotional experience that validates privilege. . . . Feverish worry over that awful African warlord. But close to 1.5 million Iraqis died from an American war of choice. Worry about that."[2]

These two complaints call into question the real reason that someone would want to be involved in these sorts of political causes. Perhaps slacktivism and the white savior industrial complex really represent shallow self-interest wrapped in moral well-wishing and spread through persuasive cosmopolitan rhetoric. But Cole's criticism fails to recognize that concern for the situation in Central Africa and apprehension about the US invasion of Iraq (an equally complicated geopolitical problem) are not mutually exclusive. And the sarcastic remark about the "awful African warlord" is not a denial that Kony is awful. Rather, it is a comment about the nature of our newfound interest in this cause, especially when something resembling a propaganda video was necessary to wake us up. Still, if these sorts of efforts bring attention to a problem that has existed in the shadows for too long, does it really matter if people also feel good about themselves by being involved? If the cumulative effect of slacktivism is actual political change (which is certainly possible when political leaders like President Obama take notice of the Kony 2012 campaign), then what is the harm if these so-called slackers feel good about participating in a righteous cause?

In the previous chapter we discussed the limits of moral argument. A perfectly logical argument is not always enough to motivate me to change my behavior, even if I recognize its merit. One natural response to this predicament is to appeal to the heart instead of the head. Emotional appeals provide the motivating force that is missing in logical, but practically inert, arguments. Take, for instance, our own country's history of racial injustice. It is no coincidence that the greatest civil rights leader in our country's history, Martin Luther King Jr., used forceful rhetoric,[3] instead of relying on his cosmopolitan ideas that "injustice anywhere is a threat to justice everywhere." Notice that those ideas alone would have meant nothing unless they were a part of a campaign of direct action to win the hearts and minds of Americans. The violent images of the Jim Crow South surely did more to end segregation than any philosophical idea. The very point of the kind of civil disobedience that Gandhi and King practiced was to force the perpetrators of violence, and society in general, to reflect on the fact that they were abusing people who were not fighting back.

Sometimes forceful rhetoric can be used in a way that seems very different from King's approach. In 1895 Booker T. Washington masterfully delivered his "Atlanta Exposition Address."[4] This speech is sometimes pejoratively called the "Atlanta Compromise Speech," since Washington adopts a surprisingly conciliatory tone in his speech to a crowd of white southern businessmen. He points out the foolishness of agitating for civil rights, even calling it the "extremest folly." He is not impressed by the cold logic of the law, which is merely a way of artificially forcing equality on a segregated South. Changing the hearts and minds of southerners requires a patient campaign of hard work and economic, rather than political, opportunity. Washington's speech is replete with emotional language, portraying his own people as "tirelessly loyal" and reminding the audience who was there for them through the years. Washington's critics, W. E. B. DuBois in particular, advanced a variety of sophisticated criticisms of his approach.[5] Still, Washington's effective use of rhetoric is undeniable. Although his strategy was different from Dr. King's, so was the society in which he lived. Washington soberly recognized the conditions of that society, and he knew that economic opportunity would provide a strong foundation for those only recently freed from slavery.

His ultimate moral and political goal was the same as Dr. King's: full and equal civil rights.

If one is fighting for a good cause, there is no problem with using emotional appeals and graphic images as the means to obtaining a righteous end. Still, when it comes to promoting a cosmopolitan ideal, a fine line exists between honestly representing the situation of those who go hungry and sensationalizing it for the sake of manipulating the heart and the wallet. That is the danger of emotional appeals and graphic images. Take, for example, the rise of ABC's hugely popular show *Extreme Makeover: Home Edition*. It would be absurd to criticize the idea of giving beautifully renovated homes to the destitute, disabled, and orphaned. Not until you dig deeper into the premise of the show might you find a reason to be critical. For instance, it might be relevant to know that a number of families featured on the show lost their recently renovated homes due to foreclosure; elaborate renovation projects seem to generate vastly increased property taxes and utility bills.

Even if this weren't the case, and even if every family lived happily ever after, the emotional manipulation at the heart of the show would still be cause for concern. The obvious product placements raise the question of whether it is better understood as an infomercial. And while some might say that the needy family spends its free vacation at Disney World because it is the happiest place on earth, perhaps the real reason is the synergy between ABC and Disney, different divisions of the same company. Perhaps this kind of corporate profit is fair compensation for doing good deeds in the community. The question, though, is whether simply doing a good thing is good enough.

This debate in ethics is an old one. Claiming that one must do the right thing for the right reason might sound like an attempt to dig too deeply into murky human psychology. Yet a few simple examples show how much this matters. Take, for instance, a college student about to graduate who is anxious about her future. One of her friends, the first in her small group to do so, gets a high-paying job and wants to take everyone else out to dinner. Is this an unequivocally good action? Or does it matter how the fortunate friend picks up the check? Even something as seemingly innocent as a tone of voice might change the action itself: "No, no, I can get it. After all, I just got that job! And I know that you all are still looking, and I just know that you'll get some good news soon." In this case, the people who benefit from a nice gesture might take offense at it.

This same question can be posed when considering whether manipulating potential donors with rhetoric and graphic images is morally acceptable. If we are concerned that the poor have been deprived of their dignity, it would be ironic if we disrespected the dignity of potential donors by using them (or their wallets) to return some of the dignity that the poor have had stolen away. Notice that we would not have to lie to anyone. We could carefully orchestrate an event designed to manipulate donors emotionally. Some might say that this complaint is not serious. If promoting solidarity amounts to getting the wealthy to give to the poor—if it is just a simple transfer of wealth—then anything we do in pursuit of that bottom line will be justified. Still, something about the term "solidarity" suggests that we are raising more than cash. It implies that we are also attempting to raise consciousness, and that cannot be done through manipulation.

Consider the case of Charles Dickens's *A Christmas Carol*. This classic tale recounts the spiritual conversion of Ebenezer Scrooge, the millionaire curmudgeon who finally appreciates the true meaning of Christmas. The story concludes with the following line: "Many laughed to see this alteration in him, but he let them laugh and little heeded them, for he knew that no good thing in this world ever happened, at which some did not have their fill of laughter. His own heart laughed and that was quite enough for him. *And it was always said of him that he knew how to keep Christmas well if any man alive possessed the knowledge.*"[6] Notice that there is no mention of Scrooge's millions. What makes him unique is the special knowledge of the Christmas spirit that he alone possesses. Only Scrooge has been confronted with the various Christmas ghosts that call into question everything he knows. His conversion not only makes him a generous millionaire but also gives him an understanding of Christmas second to none. Would the story be worth anything at all if it ended with

Scrooge simply writing a check instead of having a profound moral experience?

The authenticity of Scrooge's conversion is never questioned in the classic tale, but real life is always more complicated than fiction. Sometimes appealing to the heart can lead not only to a generous donation but also to an attempt to establish a kind of selfless mentality that claims to be authentic solidarity. But what if the supposedly selfless character is actually egoism in disguise? One could imagine a real-life Scrooge who genuinely believed that his new generosity was a sign of altruism, when in fact it was just another manifestation of his ever-present ego. This suppression of the ego (i.e., the attempt to live selflessly) is consistent with one interpretation of the Christian command to be of service to others. One of the most profound messages in the Gospels is found in Matthew 16:24: "If any want to become my followers, let them deny themselves and take up their cross and follow me." True believers do not follow half-heartedly, and the ethic of self-denial at the heart of this Gospel message has often been promoted as a moral goal.

Yet solidarity seems somehow strangely self-affirming and other-affirming at the same time. To ignore this point is, ironically, to venture into a kind of egotism completely at odds with the spirit of solidarity. A good example of this dilemma can be found in J. D. Salinger's *Franny and Zooey*.[7] Franny is a bright and sensitive college student who is completely dissatisfied by the sheer selfishness and conformity she sees in her own society. She is disgusted by the fake pursuit of knowledge and the fake concern for others. Her response to the decline of modern society is to embrace a kind of no-ego philosophy. She is inspired by Eastern philosophy to renounce desire in order to avoid (as best she can) the suffering that her less perceptive peers would experience were they not so busy living fake lives. Her no-ego ethic is motivated by a deep hope to live authentically and to avoid the daily diversions that waste the time and even the lives of those around her.

The problem with this view is that the person who tries to live selflessly in that way is simply self-deceived. Franny is no doubt the most judgmental and least tolerant character in the book, using her newfound ethic to judge everyone else as selfish and superficial; only she is enlightened. Even worse, she is forced by her own philosophical views to live as a hypocrite. After all, we cannot help but develop our own views and personalities through a unique set of experiences. We are, inevitably and ineradicably, individuals. Franny simply utters what Dr. King, in his famous "Letter from a Birmingham Jail," called "pious irrelevancies" and "sanctimonious trivialities."[8] Beautiful phrases like "we are all brothers and sisters" or "solidarity means pure selflessness" might sound meaningful, but they potentially deny the reality of individual differences and individual suffering. In so doing, they tempt us to transform our human compassion into an inhuman pity: we risk seeing those in need as mere opportunities to display our own generosity. In our misguided search for oneness with others, we reduce them to mere extensions of our own ego. We forget the fine line between charity and a charity case.

This lesson can be learned in simple but profound ways. Take, for instance, the horrific injury that Marcus Lattimore endured when he was a star University of South Carolina running back. He suffered extensive ligament damage when his knee took a direct hit during a game. Willis McGahee suffered an almost identical injury in 2003, but he overcame it to have an excellent pro career. When asked what advice he had for young Marcus, McGahee seemed surprised and even insulted by the question: "What for? So people can feel sorry for you? That don't work."[9] The author of the story points out that Lattimore "needed determination, not compassion."[10] Imagine the number of sincere well-wishers who contacted him to encourage his rehabilitation. McGahee's experience should give such fans pause: "When I got hurt, I didn't want to hear from anybody outside of my family," he said. "The only thing I can do is show him it can be done. Look at me, I did it."[11] McGahee did not want to show disrespect to Lattimore by showing him pity or seeing him as a victim of circumstance. He declined the opportunity to make himself a media darling with a tearful message to young Marcus. Instead, he taught Lattimore by example the cruel but inspiring fact that only the supposed victim can determine his fate.

Another example appears in a poem by Gerard Manley Hopkins called "Spring and Fall: To a Young Child":

Margaret, are you grieving
Over Goldengrove unleaving?
Leaves, like the things of man, you
With your fresh thoughts care for, can you?
Ah! As the heart grows older
It will come to such sights colder
By and by, nor spare a sigh
Though worlds of wanwood leafmeal lie;
And yet you will weep and know why.
Now no matter, child, the name:
Sorrow's springs are the same.
Nor mouth had, no nor mind, expressed
What heart heard of, ghost guessed:
It is the blight man was born for,
It is Margaret you mourn for.[12]

The poem is admittedly difficult to decipher. One way of interpreting it is to say that Margaret is anticipating her own mortality when she witnesses the death of all the leaves in fall. This feeling will fade over time, and the passing of the seasons will soon seem normal. Yet something is fundamentally selfish about Margaret's way of mourning, too: what seems like an empathetic and precocious act might be, at root, self-concerned ("It is Margaret you mourn for"). Even if we no longer mourn the passing of the leaves, how many of us truly take to heart the idea that "there but for the grace of God, go I"? How much of our mourning is genuinely about the person affected, and how much of it is disguised concern for ourselves?

How many times have we, in a genuine search for meaning, constructed elaborate rationalizations for why bad things happen to good people? Are we really so different from Margaret when we do this? One possible example is the tragic case of Brendon Colliflower and Samantha Kelly, beloved star athletes killed in a car crash on their prom night. Their Williamsport, Maryland, teams dedicated their respective baseball and volleyball seasons to their former leaders. Both teams won their state championships, prompting many to speculate that Brendon and Samantha's lives had fulfilled a higher purpose. The head volleyball coach said, "It was almost like that was her purpose, to make people look at life in a different way, to understand it's bigger than any one of us."[13] This is a nice sentiment, and it is a valuable way of coping with loss, but why do we feel the need to explain what might be either simply absurd or beyond the scope of human comprehension? In other words, even if there is a divine purpose behind an event that seems so senseless, why should we believe for a moment that we could understand it? It looks like we are adopting a kind of egoless perspective when we mourn in this way, when in fact we might be putting our own ego at the forefront. Why believe that the accidental death of an innocent person has a higher purpose, and further that the purpose is to instruct me?

Arthur Schopenhauer, a fascinating and underappreciated nineteenth-century German philosopher, stressed just this sort of selfless approach in his ethical writings. Inspired by Hinduism and Buddhism, Schopenhauer confidently asserted that life is suffering, an incessant alternation between unsatisfied desire and boredom. He regarded our individual differences as the root cause of this suffering. The Veil of Maya, or the "veil of tears," refers to the illusion that the differences between us are somehow fundamental.[14] This illusion causes endless conflict, but the realization of the inevitability of suffering should motivate us to develop an empathetic and cooperative understanding in order to minimize its effects. Individuals might occupy different positions and perspectives, but the suffering of another could just as easily have been my own suffering. Schopenhauer's attempt to eradicate his ego is motivated not only by the desire to see things for what they really are but also by a deep compassion for others.

But if this kind of supposedly selfless approach can be a manifestation of egoism, for reasons we have already seen, then perhaps true solidarity does require a kind of reciprocity. At the very least it seems to require a thoughtful consideration of one's own identity, rather than a false retreat into a no-ego ethic. Even with an impassible divide between two individuals, they can still forge a connection, even a friendship in some cases. True solidarity soberly recognizes that the transfer of money in the case of charity makes this connection complicated, but it insists that a genuine connection is possible nonetheless. At no point does it require the retreat into a falsely selfless philosophy.

The opportunities to forge these kinds of connections are as abundant as the ways we can be deceived about them. Think of the wide variety of websites that offer the opportunity to contribute to others. Just by clicking on a link on thehungersite. com, you give 1.1 cups of food to the hungry. You can do this every day. Perhaps the best example of this kind of outreach is Muhammad Yunus's microcredit initiative. Yunus, the "banker to the poor," won the Nobel Peace Prize in 2006 for this innovative and small-scale effort to fight poverty. Poor people who never had access to credit can now receive small loans from people halfway around the world who wish to help them with their small business plans. In an even more basic way, social media websites like Facebook can reestablish long-neglected relation-ships and even enable new connections to be made worldwide.

Whether this promotes true bonds or just the illusion of solidarity is still an open question. This conclusion should not be surprising, since technology has always played a complicated ethical role in our lives. Does Facebook, for instance, promote solidarity or lead to greater social isolation and even loneliness? Even if clicking a link on a website provides 1.1 cups of food, and even if I can support the small business dreams of a woman in Indonesia, does any of this lead to genuine solidarity? Assum-ing the trustworthiness of the websites, it leads to actual and measurable results. And it certainly makes me feel good. But is it, simply and sadly, slacktivism?

If the critics are right, and if slacktivism runs rampant among college students and young people, how can the youthful zeal to get involved in issues of social justice be converted to genuine solidarity? And what should we make of the David Lynch quote that introduced this chapter? If we experience a "narrowing of the imagination" as we grow up, does that make us more sophisticated observers of the world around us or just more cynical? Who is self-deluded, and where does the self-delusion reside? Is it the idealistic young person out to change the world, or is it the realistic adult who sees such enthusiasm as a sign of immaturity? Although Lynch probably meant imagination in its simplest form, his insight can be applied to the idea of a moral imagination also. This concerns our ability to insert ourselves mentally into a wide variety of circumstances in order to appreciate, if only for a moment, what someone else is going through. This ability seems like a unique combination of cognitive and emotive elements. Take, for example, the classic case of telling a child that someone his age is starving in China (or whatever country you choose) who would love to eat those peas. Although the child's hatred of peas often outweighs her empathy for her fictional counterpart, the combination of rational and affective appeals might sometimes win out. It seems plausible, even to a child, that someone could be hungry enough to want those peas. But it also strikes the child as sad and even pitiful that one's hunger could put someone in that position. Cultivating a strong moral imagination is undoubtedly one of the most important reasons to encourage children to read. Their natural and near limitless capacity for imaginative thought can take on a moral force as they grow older, provided they have vividly experienced the kinds of characters whose lives they are asked to imagine. In this way, a strong and genuine moral imagination can combat the temptations of a false form of solidarity.

Lynch seems to be echoing a lesson from "The Logical Song," released in 1979 by the band Supertramp. Here are some of the lyrics:

> When I was young, it seemed that life was so wonderful,
>   a miracle, it was beautiful, magical
> And all the birds in the trees, well they'd be singing so
>   happily, joyfully, playfully, watching me
> But then they sent me away to teach me how to be sen-
>   sible, logical, responsible, practical
> And they showed me a world where I could be so
>   dependable, clinical, intellectual, cynical.

In the very same year, and also in Britain, the band Pink Floyd proclaimed a similar message on "Another Brick in the Wall (Part II)," sounding the alarm on thought control disguised as education. As we grow older, our world becomes more clearly demarcated and articulated. A child might be regarded as pure potential, whereas an adult has already circumscribed the world in significant ways. This imposes limits and responsibilities on us, but it also allows us to live as specific individuals with specific views and commitments. Education can help us expand our minds, but it also indoctrinates us into specific methods and ways of thinking that have a history. Other significant possibilities are inevitably closed off to us, in ways we might not even recognize. If this is necessary, is it also good, or is it a symptom of a dead imagination? If education is a process of learning about both the world around us and ourselves, does the discipline that this demands make us narrow and sometimes even blind?

How can we enlarge the sphere of our moral concern in ways that are genuine? Much philosophical work has been done to show how morality has emotional, rather than cognitive, roots.[15] We find that we are moved to action not by an argument but by an impassioned, empathetic response to a situation. Thinking rationally can be useful when determining the best course of action, and it can help to compile useful information, but cool reflection alone is *practically* inert. But, if this is true, how can our moral concern extend to those with whom we have no affective bonds? How can it be extended to those whom we will never meet?

This challenge is not unique to ethics. It is a political problem, too. A good example comes from debates over the proper scope of government when the United States was founded. The founding fathers had to strike the right balance between national government (which could potentially threaten the local identities of citizens) and local government (which could make the nation weak and ineffective). The key political question of the time was how to take self-interested and emotionally bonded citizens from different local societies and unify them, but not too much, in a national identity. The strong emotional bonds produced what the founding fathers called "factions," or private sorts of associations (church communities, clubs, etc.). Allegiance to such factions would always threaten to override allegiance to an abstract entity called the nation. Yet the freedom of association is a basic form of liberty. A tyrannical government could simply dissolve factions, but it could not also claim to promote the freedom of its citizens.

This precise problem was raised in *Federalist Paper #10*: "Liberty is to faction what air is to fire, an aliment without which it instantly expires. But it could not be less folly to abolish liberty, which is essential to political life, because it nourishes faction, than it would be to wish the annihilation of air, which is essential to animal life, because it imparts to fire its destructive agency."[16] The solution proposed is to allow the fires of faction to burn locally (i.e., to permit the free association of emotionally bonded individuals), but to make sure that the fires could not spread and threaten the liberty of others outside of the group. Although it would be a disaster if one private association rose to power nationally, we shouldn't conclude that such an association should not exist at all. If the government were structured in such a way to permit but limit factions, then the liberty of every citizen could be protected.

Aside from preventing the spread of factions, a new sort of national identity might be formed to counteract their affective appeal. In other words, if I consider myself a patriotic citizen of a nation, then I might not always choose the good of my private association over the good of the country. Patriotism, then, is one way of expanding emotional bonds and forming identities that are not merely local. Doing this in a genuine way is, of course, the challenge. Tyrannical regimes can flood their citizens with emotional rhetoric, leading to a Stockholm Syndrome situation in which the citizens profess to love the government that oppresses them. The bizarre videos coming of out North Korea after the death of Kim Jong-il are testament to the power of propaganda to warp the minds of unsuspecting citizens.

A less extreme case is the debate over the possibility of patriotic dissent during wartime. If patriotism does not simply mean endorsing whatever the government says, then how can we distinguish between dissent that is authentically patriotic and dissent that actually hurts the war effort by undermining the morale of troops and citizens alike? In the aftermath of the Vietnam War, returning veterans found themselves in a country deeply divided. Many US citizens believed that the United States had no business being in Southeast Asia in the first place. Some veterans were subjected to verbal and physical abuse for fighting in this conflict, and some even reported being spat on when they returned home. Spitting on soldiers returning from Vietnam is a vile act, but that doesn't answer the question of what elements of the mass protests of the Vietnam War were actually expressions of patriotic sentiment. Defining what it means to be patriotic is exceedingly complex.

A more recent example comes from debates over the idea of US citizenship and civic responsibility. Cory Booker, the young mayor of Newark, New Jersey, defended his call for higher taxes on the wealthy by appealing to a sense of civic responsibility and even patriotism. He and many others have argued that the rich have a civic duty to share their wealth, since their fortune depends in large part on the larger context that enabled them to succeed. We are not self-made men and women, so we owe a debt of gratitude (and perhaps a financial debt as well) to the massive network of relationships that constitute US society. In a speech on the campaign trail, Massachusetts senator Elizabeth Warren appealed to the existence of an "underlying social contract" to justify taxing the rich:

> There is nobody in this country who got rich on their own. Nobody. You built a factory out there—good for you. But I want to be clear. You moved your goods to market on roads the rest of us paid for. You hired workers the rest of us paid to educate. You were safe in your factory because of police forces and fire forces that the rest of us paid for. You didn't have to worry that marauding bands would come and seize everything at your factory. . . . Now look. You built a factory and it turned into something terrific or

a great idea—God bless! Keep a hunk of it. But part of the underlying social contract is you take a hunk of that and pay forward for the next kid who comes along.[17]

Booker and Warren would allow the innovators and managers to make a handsome profit. The exorbitant wealth of some of these people, though, rankles their critics. Politically, this wealth threatens to undermine US democracy by shrinking the middle class and enabling wealthy individuals to purchase speech that is supposed to be free and equal. But Republican critics caution that patriotism can be used as a convenient rationalization for political motives—in this case, an expansion of federal power and an attack on the private sphere. The notion that it is patriotic for the rich to pay more seems like a nasty form of class warfare. Services like police, fire, and so on were certainly crucial to the ongoing success of private individuals. But do the rich use these services more than the middle class? At what point can we credit the innovators and managers for wealth that would not have existed without their expertise and willingness to risk capital? Doesn't their contribution to the US economy (for example, the creation of jobs for other citizens and the considerable taxes they already pay) fulfill their patriotic duty?

If a wealthy person pays 14 percent on an income of $13.7 million,[18] while a bus driver pays 20 percent on an income of $35,000, who is really paying more? The bus driver pays $7,000 in taxes, but the millionaire pays almost $2 million. Should we judge their contribution by the percentage they pay or by the total amount of wealth taken by the government? A debate has been raging in France over President Hollande's plan to impose a 75 percent super-tax on those earning more than $1.3 million.[19] Of course, having access to 25 percent of a massive fortune still makes you rich. But at what point is the government taking too much? Should we tax the super-rich at 90 percent? If it is a question of patriotism, where does their extra civic obligation end?

This interminable debate between so-called liberals and conservatives raises questions about identity in the United States. How can we achieve the delicate balance between individual rights and civic responsibility, between private choices and the public good? The debate is meaningful because both sides want to achieve the same goals: promoting freedom, responsibility, patriotism, and so on. They simply conceive of these abstract ideals in different ways. A considerably more difficult challenge is determining the responsibility that we have to those who do not share our civic identity. The idea of being a US citizen seems, at times, like a thin connection between people who might not have much in common. This perspective is especially true when politicians invoke it like it means something obvious, exhorting individuals to hand over more of their wealth. But a general sense of solidarity (however vaguely defined) is assumed by the very idea of US citizenship. On the other hand, the idea of a shared humanity seems like an even thinner and more abstract basis for a cosmopolitan ethic.

If expanding the boundaries of affective concern for others is the recipe for forming new political identities, are there natural limits to how far this can go? Is it possible even to conceive of a world government if genuine political association is rooted in emotional bonds? Every so often we debate a new international treaty or the status of the International Criminal Court. Is it possible to outsource government in the same way that we have outsourced much of our economy? Would it be good for the world to establish a kind of Super United Nations with actual authority over the citizens of various countries? Would it be good for the United States? Which should get moral and political priority?

Aside from posing a political challenge, the significance of emotional bonds poses a significant pedagogical challenge as well. Take, for example, the irony of requiring high school and college students to do some form of community service. It seems counter to the spirit of volunteerism to require students to do this. Perhaps the argument is that students who have never been exposed to this kind of activism cannot make an informed decision about whether they would like to volunteer. Mandatory volunteerism, then, puts students in a position to make a meaningful choice about whether they genuinely want to participate. Or maybe the only justification necessary is that the school's mission emphasizes the need to serve others. By virtue of enrolling in that school, the student tacitly consents to this moral goal. Still, it would be surprising to hear a community service coordinator say that she had no stake in whether her students acquired a passion for volunteerism. The pedagogical challenge, then, is similar to the ethical and political challenges: How can teachers foster the formation of new affective bonds and empathetic attachments in their students?

One experience that shows the moral complexity of mandatory volunteerism is my time spent at St. Herman's House of Hospitality in Cleveland. My high school required fifty hours of service, but I could choose where to spend my time. Most of my time at St. Herman's was spent preparing meals for the homeless. But this is where it gets complicated. The first thing I learned was that the idea of "the homeless" is a bizarre shortcut we use for discussing actual (and complex) human beings. So if the point was to foster empathy for "the homeless," the experience was a failure. On the other hand, I learned a lot about the moral ambiguity of human relationships. Since I met and worked with actual human beings instead of an abstract idea, the experience was much richer than I anticipated. Many of the people I met were happy to have me there. They took the opportunity to explain the mistakes and the bad fortune that put them on the streets. Others, however, were not so nice, and they saw right through the charade of a kid putting in volunteer hours at a place he probably would not otherwise be.

One way that colleges have tried to drive home the pedagogical value of community service is to call it "service learning." The idea is to incorporate service to the community into the college curriculum, so that students experience theoretical, classroom-based learning and practical, community-based instruction. Terms like "community service" appear to disconnect these two forms of instruction, making it seem like work outside of the classroom has no real intellectual component. The challenge posed by this model of learning, however, is how to make service learning a genuine form of learning.

Picking up trash in a rundown neighborhood near campus is easy, and it is easy to call this "community service." But if we want to incorporate learning inside and outside of the classroom, we have to make sure it is done genuinely. Slacktivists volunteer, perhaps often, but they don't seem to learn much from this feel-good form of activism. We do not seem content simply to foster a desire to serve others, for this kind of community service is deemed to be insufficiently educational. Yet conveying the true educational value of these sorts of experiences is often difficult. Maybe this reflects the slacktivism of college professors; preaching the value of service learning is meaningless unless we devise thoughtful projects with actual intellectual content. Otherwise we risk graduating students who, for instance, raise money for war orphans in Afghanistan, even though they cannot locate that country on a map and have not read a newspaper during their time on campus.

So appeals to the heart are as effective as they are, at least sometimes, morally suspect. This is true ethically, politically, and pedagogically. That we adopt a selfless philosophy that is actually egoistic, disrespect the dignity of donors through emotional manipulation in order to restore the dignity of the poor, and believe that the way to respect another person is to deny the differences between us is tragically ironic. The false form of solidarity, this pseudo-cosmopolitanism, is tempting because it is so easy. Maybe personal experience can fortify us with the wisdom not to be deceived.

Don

I suffer from a fear of flying. Once, while en route from Cleveland to New Orleans, all of the passengers were enjoying a tasty breakfast of French toast and sausage when the meal was suddenly interrupted by the voice of the pilot from the cockpit. He had a dire message. There was a fire in the luggage compartment of the aircraft, and he was being forced to make an immediate emergency landing. Within three minutes we were to be on the ground at a nearby airport surrounded by fire trucks and emergency vehicles of every kind. Some of the passengers began to cry. My initial thought was that I may have just been told what would end my life. The pilot pleaded, "Try not to be alarmed." Since that terrible scare in the air I still fly often, including every year to Africa, but now with a greater measure of fear and trepidation. I get especially nervous if, in the middle of the flight, we get an announcement from the pilot.

On the evening of July 7, 2011, I was on an early-evening flight from Nairobi, Kenya, to Mumbai, India. The stewardess had just finished serving us a marvelous supper of roasted chicken, brown rice, vegetables, cheese, whole-grain bread, wine, and a chocolate pudding dessert. Suddenly, the supper was interrupted by the voice of the pilot. I immediately tightened up. The pilot calmed me with the words, "I just want to give you an update on our current location." He told us that we were thirty thousand feet directly above the Somali capital Mogadishu, about to begin our crossing of the Arabian Sea.

At that time, an explosive outbreak of hunger was striking those living in the Horn of Africa. Hardest hit were the people of Somalia, Ethiopia, and Kenya. Since I had been researching hunger that summer, I had been reading reports out of Somalia on a nearly daily basis. In the height of the drought that swept millions of people all across East Africa into crisis in 2011, the United Nations declared that six regions of Somalia had been plunged into famine. Malnutrition rates hovered in excess of 30 percent, and water access was less than four liters of water per person per day. The hunger situation in the capital city, Mogadishu, one of the most lawless cities on earth, was growing grimmer with each new day. The Al Qaeda–linked terrorist group al-Shabab had a stranglehold on the city, forcing many aid groups to abandon their humanitarian mission there. Thousands were fleeing from this region of Somalia every day in search of more food and greater security. Those who remained were forced to live on the scarcest of rations. Now I was right there, in such close physical proximity to one of the hungriest places on earth.

Instead of feeling less than six miles away, albeit vertically, I felt that I was 6 million miles away. My situation in the air was so dramatically different from those starving on the ground right below our plane. I feared for the people of this city. I struggled considering what I might do to connect to them in some concrete way. I wanted to be one of those helping to alleviate their suffering, but I didn't know the way. I continuously prayed for them. I continuously worried about their future.

The more I broke from my own routine to contemplate their immediate plight, the more I sensed it was *our* future for which I was praying. The words of one of my heroes, Cardinal Leo Joseph Suenens of Belgium, spoken in the early 1960s when global hunger raged on every continent, rang in my ears:

> No man of good will can accept that two out of three human beings should suffer hunger. Civilization is not worthy of its name if it remains indifferent to this social and collective sin. We are still very far from mutual understanding, from an authentic spirit of friendship. We cross paths, as we hurry along our ways, without a word or a smile. In our century, man has discovered interplanetary space, and yet we have only begun to explore that space which separates us from one another. Man has built gigantic bridges to span rivers and torrents, but we have yet to learn how to reach across the abyss that separates one people from another.[20]

Nyumbani is the first home established for HIV-positive orphans in Kenya. The word *nyumbani* is a Swahili word meaning home. It is a place where children who have seen both mother and father die of AIDS come to live because no one else has opened the door of their home or heart to them. It was at Nyumbani that we discovered firsthand how hunger is related to a whole plethora of other health crises. In our first day at Nyumbani we were inspired to learn that the volunteers and caregivers have elected not to eat meat, chicken, or fish so that these sources of nutritional strength, always more expensive than other foods, could be provided for the children. While working there I befriended a Kenyan named Moses Nyambura, a twenty-three-year-old local volunteer. He was hoping to get a paying job one day at Nyumbani. He worked extremely hard for two years before being hired as a driver.

In October 2011, as the famine raged in the northeastern region of Kenya, Moses responded to a direct appeal to join the fight to alleviate the sufferings in his homeland. The initiative he joined was known as "Kenyans for Kenya" and was jointly sponsored by the communication company Safaricom and the Kenya Red Cross. In Africa, more and more people are using their phones to transfer funds electronically to relatives and friends in need. It is the safest and fastest way for getting help to someone in immediate need of assistance. In this crisis many Kenyans were clearly being inspired to see one another other as compatriots who share a common homeland and a common destiny that are in jeopardy because of the scarcity of food. The initial goal they set for themselves was to raise a half a billion Kenyan schillings in order to provide some significant emergency food aid. This was quickly surpassed by over 1 billion schillings, in a poor region of our world where half the population live below $2 a day. Some who could afford as few as ten Kenyan schillings sent it over their phone to join the crusade.

Moses related his first impressions to me upon arriving at Turkana in northeastern Kenya:

> The big shock was to see people who were so weak and had gone days without food. They all had to walk many kilometers to get to the camp. When you first see them you are startled by all the changes in their bodies brought on by starvation. Everywhere I looked I saw sunken cheeks, shriveled skin, sagging breasts, and others whose eyesight was failing them because their whole body was so weakened by the extreme hunger. The very young and the very old seemed to suffer the worst ravages.

Moses immediately realized they had journeyed to a very desperate place where hunger was pushing people to the brink of violence, despair, or both. As they started to unload the trucks, a very long line spontaneously started to form. Some people were thrown to the ground in the press of the crowd. Moses writes:

> There was chaos and pushing as everyone wanted to be at the front. All I could see was dust as there was mayhem everywhere and people clamoring for your attention. It was very hard to bring everyone to order, but we could not distribute anything till calm was restored. When things eventually calmed down, we shared the food. Each family received six kilos of maize grain, four kilos of beans, and two kilos of porridge flour. Eventually 600 persons at the camp received immediate food supplies. The very weak had to be supported to even prepare and eat the food.

In the summer of 2011, as drought, famine, and death were stalking the Horn of Africa, I faced inner questions daily about the strength of our common resolve to feed our hungry sisters and brothers. The media too frequently offers the perspective that this monumental task is too daunting, or even intractable. The ravages of famine in East Africa were nothing new. It was the fifth major threat to food security in the region since 2000. In Ethiopia fears were mounting that the devastation there would resemble or surpass the 1984 famine, in which 1 million people died. The Kenyan government struggled to provide just the very basic services to an estimated 440,000 refugees fleeing hunger in their homelands at Dadaab Camp, a facility intended to house only 90,000 refugees.[21] Behind these grim truths lie the stories and the faces of children whose bodies are yearning for food and life even as their spirits are losing their grip on hope.

Abbas Gullet, secretary general of the Kenya Red Cross, said his organization had responded to the warning and launched an appeal in early 2011. The systemic failure, he believes, lay in the government's failure to ring official alarm bells. Only after large numbers of Kenyans became personally involved through the Kenya for Kenyans campaign were sizeable funds raised and did the attention of government become more focused on the food crisis. In the Kenya for Kenyans initiative, large numbers of individuals responded to a summons that gave to them a sense of contributing directly to the well-being of others. The Kenyan government eventually grew far more proactive, but only after a popular uprising of compassion by the masses of Kenyans who awakened these officials to their role of service in the common good. The food security that has been achieved resulted not only from personal initiatives and achievements but also clearly through the workings of community.

The food crisis in the Horn of Africa was in many ways predictable. There has been a generally reactive, rather than preemptive, focus in the international community on facing the pressing issues of famine relief. The UN Food and Agricultural Organization had warned of food insecurity in the Horn of Africa for ten months straight before others recognized the terrible onslaught. Humanitarian agencies have long lamented that the gravity of such widespread food emergencies routinely escape serious notice until startling images of parched land, dying animals, and most especially emaciated children circulate around the globe and evoke horror in us all.

The first time you encounter someone too weak even to eat is a tormenting and agonizing experience. It was a summer day in 2004 when that ordeal first entered my life. I found myself seated on the ground outside a health-care clinic in Kibera, perhaps the largest slum in Africa, located in Moses's hometown of Nairobi. I sat next to an eight-year-old girl who was waiting to receive treatment for AIDS. She was frail and feverish. Her tiny body was visibly exhausted. It was midday, and I had a piece of roasted maize as my lunch. I broke it in half and gently placed some in her hands. She smiled with gratitude. She barely had the strength to lift it to her mouth. Most of the maize went uneaten, but it was clear that she enjoyed the experience of holding warm and tasty food in her hands. She also knew that she was in the company of someone who cared about her.

The fear I related earlier of possibly dying in the plane bound for New Orleans, and the fear I had for my Somali sisters and brothers facing possible starvation directly below our plane bound for India, are not unrelated. The blessings of life I so urgently wanted to preserve for myself while I was in danger are the precise blessings that I hope sustain others in peril. No follower of Christ can draw near the sufferings of others and remain ensconced in a selfish security. Gospel living always stretches the boundaries of our lives to include the vulnerable persons whom Providence purposefully places near us, either physically or in our hearts and in our concern.

For seven years I lived and studied in Belgium, my adoptive homeland. The Catholic University of Louvain, in the heart of the region known as Flanders, is my alma mater. Its faculty of theology began teaching in 1425, making it the oldest continuously Catholic university in the world. There I first learned how war and hunger can be companions. In the 1970s I befriended an elderly Belgian couple named Felix and Emily who had been married for sixty-five years. Every Saturday morning I enjoyed fresh pastries and tea in their company. One Saturday morning, without warning them in advance, I brought a friend, a German seminarian, with me. Their behavior changed. They seemed caught off guard and visibly shaken. They would tell me later that they had not had a German in their home since their house was forcibly occupied in the war years. Felix and Emily had a living memory of their homeland twice being defeated and occupied, a memory of their home twice forced to house foreign soldiers. What they remember most of all was the hunger. They told me stories of the hardships they endured and how difficult it was for them to forgive their former enemy.

Every day I went to class in Louvain I walked down a street known as the Rue de Herbert Hoover. It ends in a huge plaza, the largest in the city, called the Hooverplein. US voters of the Depression era removed President Herbert Hoover from the presidency, ushering in the Roosevelt years. Herbert Hoover was derided by his critics for tearing society apart and increasing the gulf between the haves and the have-nots. The have-nots ended up in "Hoovervilles," the legendary shantytowns that sprouted up across the United States during the Depression. They were built by millions of people pushed into homelessness by abject poverty. At the same time, in Western Europe, major streets and impressive public squares were named after this very same man whom US citizens blamed for their personal misfortune and our collective misery.

The people of my adoptive homeland in Belgium have a much different attitude toward Herbert Hoover. One hundred years ago, in a dire time of war, October 1914, Herbert Hoover helped create the Commission for the Relief of Belgium (CRB).[22] This organization was charged with the task of organizing relief efforts to combat a severe food shortage in German-occupied Belgium and northern France in World War I. The CRB dispensed 5 million metric tons of provisions, valued at almost $3 billion, to help feed our hungry brothers and sisters. The lesson that the CRB can offer to our efforts in the twenty-first century to feed a hungry world is that it is possible, even on a massive scale, to remain efficient, accountable, all-inclusive, moral, and optimistic in devising ways to provide food security to every human being. Our grandparents and great-grandparents did it before, and we can do it again in our day with the moral and political will to act.

Later, as head of the US Food Administration, Hoover, with brilliant efficiency, organized and sent food shipments to millions of starving people affected by World War I. Hoover did not mix politics with the absolutely essential task of feeding a starving humanity. He made sure that food aid also went to the defeated Germans after the war. In another bold and controversial humanitarian act, food and relief aid was given to the famine-stricken Bolshevik-controlled region of Russia in 1921, despite enormous opposition from US politicians, Republicans and Democrats. When he was accused of helping Bolshevism, Hoover answered, "Twenty million people are starving. Whatever their politics, they shall be fed."[23] By the time the war ended, the *New York Times* named Hoover one of the "Ten Most Important Living Americans."

Hoover's bold statement, backed by action, envisioned food as a fundamental human right. Not until after World War II would the community of nations enshrine in its Universal Declaration of Human Rights in 1948 the principle that every human being, without exception, has a right to a standard of living adequate to support his or her health and well-being, including food. Appreciation is growing that we are connected with one another as members of one global community.

The great recession of 2008–2009 and the subsequent slow recovery from the economic collapse that followed made the numbers of people in the United States in need of food assistance spike dramatically. Our nation's Supplemental Nutrition Assistance Program (SNAP), an agency run by the US Department of Agriculture, saw a 70 percent rise in those seeking food help in four years. In 2007 there were 26.3 million individual SNAP recipients; by 2011, there were 44.7 million—the most dramatic rise in food assistance requests in the lifetime of most Americans. It was reminiscent of the Depression era, the direst time in the past century for families struggling to feed their children. Such a dramatic change in our common life about an issue affecting millions of people raised many reflections and concerns. On the one hand, some people question whether we are fashioning a culture of dependency wherein we ask government to do for us what we cannot or will not do for ourselves. Others see the same situation in a whole different light. Like other nations, the United States has not been spared from the economic impacts of unemployment. We witnessed a sharp rise in the unemployment rate, from 4.6 percent in 2007 to 8.9 percent in 2011. Astonishingly, some among the unemployed declined any assistance whatsoever. They were concerned that the food assistance given them might be needed for others who were potentially even more desperate than themselves. Also, they had come to believe that the federal food safety net was a measure of protection for others rather than an empowerment for their journey back to self-reliance and their ability to contribute to the commonweal. Nonetheless, SNAP extends opportunity to some of the most vulnerable in our communities, helping create the kind of health and strength that every person needs to embrace life.

Combating hunger remains the first and most essential step toward building thriving communities. I have seen the suffering of the hungry firsthand in my work at the Westside Catholic Center in Cleveland. One person in particular comes to mind. She was thirty-eight years old and clinically fearful of just about everyone. Her face, despite the permanent scar left by a terrible knife wound, remained beautiful. Her home was an alcove of a bank building in the bustling commercial center of downtown Cleveland. Freda was her name, although she seldom had the joy of hearing anyone call her by name. She was just one more face lost in the crowd of people daily passing by on the streets of this large city. I couldn't help but notice that she was always alone and frequently depressed.

She would one day come to trust me enough to tell me that she had suffered from mental illness and had been plagued with suicidal thoughts most of her adult life. She just did not know how to communicate her deep need for others. The highlight of Freda's day was the warm lunch she enjoyed at the West Side Catholic Center. There she encountered the only people she ever grew to trust, or at least trust a little: the volunteers who daily staff this drop-in center. These volunteers range in age from ten to eighty-eight years old. Together, they possess the gift of creating an atmosphere where each person senses he or she is welcomed, and even prized.

In this place of hospitality, the interconnectedness of our lives is clearly visible. Volunteers from the suburbs mingle with people whose worry that day is to find a warm and safe place to sleep that night. People whose lives are played out in hidden places—under bridges and freeway overpasses, inside abandoned cars and buildings—share conversation with others whose lifestyle is marked by comfort and security. Volunteers come to the West Side Catholic Center with the expectation that they will prepare lunch, sort and distribute clothes, and provide child care. What really happens is that a personal bond begins to grow between them and the people they serve. Life-giving and life-affirming friendships form here between members of two diverse groups we routinely call the rich and the poor. Even Freda, with all her fears, felt safe and at home in this welcoming community.

Freda did not survive the cruelty of last winter's life on the streets. She was stabbed again—this time in the heart, not her face. An estimated two-thousand-plus people live outdoors each winter in Cleveland, and about fifty of them do not survive another year. Many die alone on the street, like Freda, a victim of random, deadly violence. Whenever one of us dies alone, unloved and unmourned, another thread is being plucked out of the fabric that holds the human family together.

Near the intersection of Green and Harvard Roads in Highland Hills, Ohio, a simple paved road leads back to a verdant field surrounded by a golf course and what some describe as a garbage dump. Since approximately 1904, this land has been reserved as a potter's field, a burial place for unknowns and bottom-of-the-ladder folk who die in our midst. Several thousand people have been buried here in unmarked graves over the course of nearly a century. It appears to be a place deliberately concealed. The simple wooden gate that once marked the entrance is gone. This place we have designated as holy ground has become obscure and hard to find.

The first time I went to the cemetery where Freda is buried, I drove past the entrance three times. There was no marker, no road sign, no indication whatsoever that this attractive field of lush green grass was a graveyard. If you are destitute in Greater Cleveland, so destitute that neither you nor your family can afford to purchase a grave, you will be buried here in this open field. If you die in a tenement, on the street, or under a freeway overpass, and no one claims you, you will be interred in this hard-to-find place. If you live and die like Freda, this is your final resting place. In the depth of winter, it's peculiarly lonely. You will find no footprints in the snow as evidence of any remembrance by others of the lives interred here. Every time I leave Potter's Field, I depart wondering if, in our civic memory, we are ashamed that some of us die this way. Is that why we attempt to deliberately hide a part of who we are as a community?

A fundamental moral measure of any society is how the poor and vulnerable are faring. The burial place of the forgotten poor who have died in Greater Cleveland is an unmarked field. Regrettably, they are not the only ones forgotten. At the same time, among the living, today's children are the ones most in danger of sharing the same fate: forgotten and lost in a world of neglect. An estimated nearly 200 million homeless children live in our world. While they live predominantly in the countries of the Southern Hemisphere, in the United States today our young also are among the most vulnerable. Why is it that the younger you are in America, the more likely you are to be poor? Indeed, 25 percent of our preschool children are growing up poor in a land of plenty. They are trapped in living graveyards, almost as if a collective judgment has been silently made that the children of the poor are "disposable"; their future warrants no serious discussion.

Potter's Field has only one acknowledgment that it is holy ground. A large stone in the field bears on it a verse from St. John's Gospel: "Peace I leave with you, my peace I give unto you. Let not your heart be troubled, neither let it be afraid." In a compassionate society, in a nation of greatness, there are moral attachments to one another that are never denied, in life and in death. I will never cease thanking God that Freda experienced some measure of human solidarity at the West Side Catholic Center, and for Freda's trusting me with the gift of herself. Freda, her life and death, have a rightful place in our civic memory.

Notes

¹ Laura Rozen, "Kony 2012 Filmmaker Jason Russell Speaks Out: 'We Can All Agree We Can Stop [Kony] This Year,'" Yahoo News online, March 9, 2012, http://news.yahoo.com.

² Ibid.

³ To recognize the significance of King's rhetoric, and not just his ideas, trying reading a copy of his famous "I Have a Dream" speech and then watch the video. The text alone is moving, but the video has no comparison. Martin Luther King Jr., "I Have a Dream," collected in *I Have a Dream: Writings and Speeches That Changed the World* (New York: HarperOne, 2003), 83–100.

⁴ The full text is available in *Great Speeches by African Americans*, ed. James Daley (Mineola, NY: Dover, 2006), 81–85.

⁵ See especially chapter 3 ("Of Mr. Booker T. Washington and Others") in W. E. B. DuBois, *The Souls of Black Folk* (New York: Tribeca Books, 2013).

⁶ Charles Dickens, *A Christmas Carol: The Original Manuscript* (Oxford: Benediction Classics, 2012), 151, emphasis added.

⁷ J. D. Salinger, *Franny and Zooey* (New York: Little, Brown, 1991).

⁸ Martin Luther King Jr., "Letter from a Birmingham Jail," in *I Have a Dream: Writings and Speeches That Changed the World* (New York: HarperOne, 2003), 83–100.

⁹ Jason Cole, "Direct Snap: Willis McGahee Is a Good Model for Marcus Lattimore; Just Don't Ask for His Advice," Yahoo Sports, November 1, 2012.

¹⁰ Ibid.

¹¹ Ibid.

¹² Gerard Manley Hopkins, "Spring and Fall: To a Young Child," in *Gerard Manley Hopkins: The Major Works* (New York: Oxford University Press), 152.

¹³ Chris Ballard, "Winning for Sam," *Sports Illustrated*, December 3, 2012.

¹⁴ Arthur Schopenhauer's masterwork is *The World as Will and Representation*, 2 vols. trans. E. F. J. Payne (Mineola, NY: Dover, 1969).

¹⁵ David Hume (1711–1776) is perhaps the most famous example of a philosopher who claims that morality is rooted in the passions, rather than reason. See especially his *Enquiries Concerning Human Understanding and Concerning the Principles of Morals* (New York: Oxford University Press, 1975).

¹⁶ Federalist #10, in *The Federalist Papers*, ed. Clinton Rossiter (Seattle: Signet, 1982).

¹⁷ Lucy Madison, "Elizabeth Warren: 'There Is Nobody in This Country Who Got Rich on His Own,'" CBS News, September 22, 2011, http://www.cbsnews.com.

¹⁸ These figures, though hotly contested, were roughly what presidential candidate Mitt Romney had to defend when he released his 2011 tax returns. See Jeanne Sahadi, "Romney Paid 14% Effective Tax Rate in 2011," *CNNMoney*, November 21, 2012.

¹⁹ France's Constitutional Council struck down the president's plan, but he has revamped it to apply to companies instead of individuals. See Scott Saraye, "French Council Strikes Down 75% Tax Rate," *New York Times*, December 30, 2012.

²⁰ Cardinal Leo Joseph Suenens, *Memories and Hopes* (Dublin: Veritas, 1992), 104.

²¹ Mark Tran, "Somalia Famine: Refugees Move into Dadaab Extension," *The Guardian*, October 2, 2011.

²² The Belgian American Educational Foundation offers a clear and concise history of the CRB at http://www.baef.be/documents/about-us/history/the-commission-for-relief-in-belgium-1914-.xml?lang=en.

²³ As quoted by Terry Golway, "Humanizing Hoover," *New York Observer*, January 7, 2009.

Chapter 4

The Value of Personal Experience

> We're all going to die, all of us, what a circus! That alone
> should make us love each other, but it doesn't. We are
> terrorized and flattened by trivialities. We are eaten up
> by nothing.
>
> —*Charles Bukowski*[1]

Jim

Fyodor Dostoevsky's novel *The Idiot* includes a captivating
scene in which the main character tells the story of a man condemned to die. While marching to face the firing squad, a beautiful
and terrifying thought occurs to him: "What if I didn't have to die?
What if I could get my life back—what an infinity it would be!
And it would all be mine! Then I would make each minute into
a whole lifetime, I would lose nothing, would account for each
minute, waste nothing in vain!"[2] The man was so overcome by the
thought that he wished they would shoot him as soon as possible
to give him some relief from his insight. At the last minute, his
sentence was shockingly commuted, and that is where the storyteller abruptly ends his account. The unsatisfied audience demands
to know whether the freed man actually embraced the infinity he
had been granted. The storyteller absentmindedly responds, "Oh
no, he told me himself—I'd already asked him about it—he didn't
live like that at all, and wasted far too many minutes."[3]

The freed man cannot be blamed for his inability to live according to his crushing insight. A feature of human nature that

is too often ignored is the fact that we tend to be habitually forgetful creatures. Despite the sheer number of opportunities we stumble upon to live more reflective and empathetic lives, the force of habit manages to overcome our best efforts to change. This is not a simple case of moral failure but a deeply rooted part of who and what we are. Having a consistent identity of any kind presupposes the continuity of past and present. Habit keeps us sane. It provides a basic structure and framework for the way we experience the world. Yet, as the French philosopher Michel de Montaigne cautions us, "Habit puts to sleep the eye of judgment."[4]

Succumbing to the easy comfort of habit can mean that we no longer actively evaluate ourselves and the world around us with a critical eye. As the Bukowski quote suggests, we squander the simple wisdom we might gain by acknowledging our own (and others') mortality. And we do this not for some profound reason but because we become "terrorized and flattened by trivialities." We trade the possibility of true insight into the human condition for the anxiety of daily tasks that have no lasting meaning. For the most part, this is done unconsciously, or at least not in full awareness of the terrible bargain into which we enter. We are consoled, like the character in *The Idiot*, by infinitely small accomplishments and the assurance that we won't have to reflect more deeply on the meaning of our lives. Perhaps we sleepwalk through life instead of genuinely living it, missing opportunities to remedy injustice or to simply enjoy and appreciate our immense good fortune.

Consider the case of someone who believes that we live in a postracial society, where race no longer serves as a primary source of identity and difference between individuals. The habit of self-consciously treating people as individuals rather than representatives of their race may conceal a deeper sort of self-deception. Maybe this person explicitly and repeatedly affirms his postracial beliefs, but he also crosses the street when encountering someone of a different race whom he perceives to be a possible threat. It would be unfair to regard this person simply as a racist, but there might be an element of racial prejudice of which even he is not consciously aware. Even perfectly moral habits (i.e., the conscious attempt to transcend race in daily interactions) can, over time, erode our critical sense. We might deny the existence of problems, not because they have been solved, but because we cannot see them anymore.

A different type of example might be a version of what is known in economics as the "law of diminishing returns." We can become so accustomed to a pleasant and wished-for state of affairs that we appreciate it less. When I first moved to Atlanta to attend graduate school in August 2003 I was grateful not to have to deal with the heavy snow and bitter cold of Cleveland. But, after a while, it was only in conversation with family back home that I was even reminded of this. Having moderate winter weather became customary, and my gratitude turned into disappointment when we would have the occasional frost. On one trip home I found myself unprepared to deal with the cold that used to be completely normal.

Those with a fine-tuned critical sense fight, often fruitlessly, against the sedative effect of habit. As the German poet Goethe remarked, "There is nothing harder to bear than a succession of sunny days." A poet who relies upon his ability to stay awake and offer new and interesting insights into the human experience must regard habit as a burden, especially when it is a "succession of sunny days." An occasional sunny day is a joy, but becoming accustomed to good weather threatens our ability to appreciate it. The ancient philosopher Epicurus offered a similar insight. Contrary to the contemporary connotation of the word "Epicurean," the philosopher Epicurus recommended stringent restrictions on indulgence. He insisted that one could be just as satisfied with a diet of bread and water as one would be with a diet full of rich food and drink. It simply depended on what one was accustomed to. Once one was accustomed to an ordinary diet, an occasional feast would be that much more memorable. I learned this lesson after overindulging at one of my favorite restaurants in Atlanta. Several times a week, I ordered a lunch special called the Mediterranean Feast. It was, indeed, a feast, and it was delicious. Then the restaurant unexpectedly closed for renovations, and I found myself sorely disappointed. I realized two things: first, that I had not enjoyed the food in quite the same way after a few weeks of eating it, and second, that despite this fact, my disappointment upon learning of the renovations was completely unwarranted for such a minor inconvenience.

The story from *The Idiot* is surprising because it is seems like such an extreme example. Yet many other moments in life hold similar promise. Ten years ago I visited Uganda for the first time. When I returned home, everything felt foreign, and the world seemed different—but only for a few weeks. Life inevitably goes back to normal. Eight years later I returned to Uganda, this time sure that life would be different. After another incredible experience I was once again profoundly grateful for the privileges I had been granted throughout my life. Once again, this gratitude passed, as a life that had once been stirred up began to settle. I can already feel my more recent trip to India dissolve into the fog of memory.

Perhaps we can keep memories fresh in our hearts and minds if we surround ourselves with reminders of the past. An artifact from a life-changing trip can be regarded as an experience or a moment in time embodied in an object. Yet this artifact can also become a souvenir, prized as an object rather than a memory incarnate. For instance, I brought an African drum home from my first trip to Uganda. I have a strong memory of driving up to the roadside stand, seeing the drum makers practicing their craft, and watching the hilarity of an African negotiation ensue. Now the drum sits on a bookcase, an object among others. The beautiful African *batik* (a kind of decorative wall hanging) that adorns my office is an object of curiosity to visitors, and it fits the color scheme. But it does not evoke the memories it once did.

Objects on a mantel retain a residue of emotion, but they blend into the background of busy lives. Taken out of the original context that gave them meaning, they are like trophy fish extracted from the sea and mounted on a wall. The European fascination with the "exotic" character of African art in the early twentieth century provides us with a compelling example of this phenomenon. What might be called African art was originally designed to be functional and to play a specific and practical role in the life of the community. Understanding these works of art merely as aesthetically pleasing objects misrepresents their actual significance. Displaying such objects in a museum in an attempt to elevate them to high art is, ironically, a way of sentencing them to death.

Even if we could surround ourselves with objects that always remind us of what we once experienced, simply having a vivid memory of something does not determine *how* we are to think about it. For instance, a meaningful encounter with a homeless person might motivate us to help the homeless in general (if we are willing to generalize, inventing a category of thought called "homeless people," from one or several experiences). But this does not begin to answer the question of how we are to help *them* and whether the same obligation can be applied uniformly across all cases. Are we obligated to give money to the homeless, or are we obligated to withhold money and direct them to a shelter where they can receive more reliable support? In this case, claiming we have deep moral obligations to one another settles nothing about their actual character.

While personal experience can undeniably offer insight into the suffering of others, the way this suffering is remembered and commemorated is complicated. Our enduring memories all pertain to particular persons and events; I have no memory of Africa or India as overall experiences, but many specific memories of the people and places we visited. So even the insight gained through personal experience is limited in the same way as our experience of the world in general. Inferring that one grasps the nature of our obligations to those in need just because one has personally experienced a few instances of that need might be shortsighted. Memory deals with what is unique and irreplaceable rather than common and generic.

The Argentine author Jorge Luis Borges (1899–1986) wrote a fascinating short story called "Funes, His Memory" that illustrates this exact problem concerning memory. Following a fall from a horse, the main character is blessed (or cursed) with the ability to remember every moment of his life in perfect detail. Borges writes, "[Funes] knew the forms of the clouds in the southern sky on the morning of April 30, 1882, and he could compare them in his memory with the veins in the marbled binding of a book he had seen only once, or with the feathers of spray lifted by an oar on the Rio Negro on the eve of the Battle of Quebracho."[5] Funes relished his newfound ability, but he seemed blissfully unaware of the trade-off it forced him to make. "He had effortlessly learned English, French, Portuguese, Latin. I suspect, nevertheless, that he was not very good at thinking. To think is to ignore (or forget) differences, to generalize, to abstract. In the teeming world of Ireneo Funes there was nothing but par-ticulars—and they were virtually *immediate* particulars."[6] Making sense of our memories requires an act of reflection, given that memories do not and cannot interpret themselves. These reflec-tions can change over time, as we gain the critical distance neces-sary for assessing them.

A good example of this is the time I was interrogated by an older man constructing a small house in Uganda. I was walking to breakfast one morning when this man called me over and asked if I had ever built a house. I responded that I hadn't but that his project looked very good. He pointedly asked me why I didn't do some real work and "bake in the sun" with him and his crew. Why did I spend so much time reading inside? Not knowing what to say to this provocation (or was it an honest attempt to bond?), I shyly repeated my praise of his construction skills and went on my way. But before I could leave, the man said that he knew I was visiting schools and distributing scholarship money. He described in detail his difficult life and wondered if there was money available for him, too.

I was immediately bothered by this confrontation. I felt an-gry at being called out for a soft and decadent lifestyle, guilty when he discussed his lifelong lack of opportunity, and confused when the man insulting me also solicited money. I suspect that he saw me as a cash cow *and* as an object of ridicule. While this is probably not a rare combination, seldom is it expressed so can-didly. Should I have joined him for some hard labor every day of my visit before returning to my privileged life? Would that have

proven something, or would I have been merely posing as someone in solidarity? Would I have earned the respect or ridicule of
the man and his crew? What was the appropriate response to this
aggressive invitation? The truth is that I was not baking in the sun because I didn't
have to. Barring some unforeseen circumstances, I never would.
He, however, would likely spend the rest of his days doing what
he was doing just then, and he recognized this explicitly. Even
that assumes he is fortunate enough to find work consistently. Is
this vivid memory an invitation to be in solidarity or a reminder
of our fundamentally different situations? Was this man providing me with insight into the human condition, or was he simply
being rude?

Two years later, a visit to a slum in Mumbai, India, provided more memories that require interpretation in order to
be meaningful. Visiting a slum might equally foster a desire for
solidarity and an attitude of resignation upon witnessing the
enormity of the problem of poverty. Seeing the pure joy on the
faces of the children at school was inspiring beyond belief, and
the colorful dresses worn by their devoutly committed teachers
surely stand out in my mind. But I also remember the contrast
between the intricately patterned dresses and the endless muck
that sucked at our shoes as we walked through the slum. And
it is hard to believe that education will prove to be a ticket out
of a life of poverty, especially when the degree of desperation
is this high.

In her riveting account of life in a Mumbai slum, Katherine
Boo reveals the moral complexity at the heart of slum living.
Although the subtitle of her book is *Life, Death, and Hope in a
Mumbai Undercity*, most of Boo's account seems utterly devoid of
hope.[7] The daily struggle to survive is exacerbated by corruption
so basic and endemic that it seems impossible to root out, yet
her thoughtful and fully human descriptions of the children she
met makes reading this book a little bewildering. I am reminded
of the psychologist's image of a duck/rabbit: seen in one way,
the image is clearly a duck, but all you have to do is shift your
perspective slightly to see it as a rabbit.

Boo's book has the same effect: Is the protagonist, Abdul, a sullen child condemned by fate and the corruption of the justice system to rot in prison for a crime he didn't commit? Or is he a persevering young man who wants nothing more than to maintain his integrity and to be the best version of himself (to "be like ice," even though he realizes that he is more like "dirty water")? Under these conditions, Abdul's normal human behavior (e.g., his refusal to cheat someone in his garbage-sorting business) takes on a superhuman quality. Boo doesn't say what ultimately happens to him, leaving his fate as open-ended as our interpretation of his character.

Aside from the indeterminate interpretations of our experience, memory itself is often random and haphazard, rather than a reliable account of our personal experience. For every precious memory of a person or place I have visited, I find myself with one or several memories that are just as fresh and utterly irrelevant. I remember the impromptu—and tearful—conversation I had with a nun who personally witnessed the abduction of many of her students by Joseph Kony's forces (the brutal rebel leader of the Lord's Resistance Army in Uganda). But I also recall what I had for breakfast that morning. And I cannot seem to remember a specific conversation with a teacher that, at the time, I thought I would treasure forever.

I remember the only stereotypically tourist activity we did in Uganda: visiting a game park. It was incredible to see all the animals simultaneously turn their attention to the predator that was, as our guide told us, slinking through the tall grass. But I also recall how much of my energy and effort that day was spent trying to stand in the back of a jeep and take pictures without breaking my cheap camera. While those pictures remind me of the actual experience, they sometimes also seem like voyeuristic artifacts. I wonder how much more rich and fulfilling the experience would have been if I had not seen it through a viewfinder. Would I remember the smells and sounds? Would I have noticed something in my peripheral vision that forever escaped my attention?

We cannot prepare ourselves for meaningful experiences that simply happen spontaneously, nor can we always recall those experiences as well as we would like. In his *Discourse on Method*, René Descartes identifies a similar problem with the way we write historical accounts. He pays a series of backhanded compliments to the various subjects he was forced to study in school, criticizing history for being insufficiently scientific: "And even the most accurate histories, if they neither alter nor exaggerate the significance of things in order to render them more worthy of being read, almost always at least omit the baser and less noteworthy details."[8] Historical accounts, in Descartes' view, either consciously or unintentionally deceive us. But to say that our memories require interpretation to become meaningful is not to say anything new. It just means that one should recognize that personal experience, no matter how meaningful, does not itself determine the stories we tell ourselves and others.

This point is brought to life in an ancient philosophical dispute: the difference between the Epicurean and the Stoic attitudes toward memory. Epicurus promoted the cultivation of one's memory, so that one could literally "reexperience" the beautiful moments of one's life when dealing with hardship.[9] He even reported being happy on his own deathbed: his ability to call to mind certain moments of his past combated not only the psychological pain of dying, but, perhaps improbably, the physical pain as well. He regarded philosophy as a form of spiritual exercise that required much patience and practice, much like an athlete must constantly train in order to be fit.

Epicurus's philosophical enemies, the Stoics, similarly taught the value of spiritual exercise, but they did so to remind themselves of the fleeting character of the present moment. In other words, if Epicurus's philosophy is an attempt to preserve the fleeting nature of memories, the Stoic philosophy is an attempt to recognize those memories precisely as fleeting. Doing so would reduce the emotional attachments that can cause pain, anxiety, and regret, either by holding onto a painful experience now long past or by focusing on a happy memory similarly buried in time.

Even if one could cultivate one's memory in order to have richer personal experiences, should this result in Epicurus's imaginative and empathetic attachment to the past, or Stoicism's recognition that such an attachment can just as easily be a source of pain? To return to the question posed earlier: Is the memory of a devastating visit to a slum in Mumbai a call for greater solidarity with those in tremendous need, or is it a reminder of the intractable nature of global poverty? The memory of the experience cannot answer the question on its own. Personal experience alone cannot determine the scope of our obligation to others if it is overpowered by the force of habit, the difficulty of generalizing from unique experiences, and the fact that memory—however vivid—does not determine how we are to respond to it.

Don

The human family is rapidly growing, expanding by roughly 83 million persons each year. The demand for water in our cities and countryside is increasing in much the same proportion. Fears are mounting that some communities and nations will hoard water in a way that harms us all. Many nations, especially in regions plagued by severe water scarcity, view water security more and more as a vital national security issue. In recent years, numerous nongovernmental organizations have sprouted up attempting to pressure governments to establish water-sharing commitments and build a more cooperative spirit in order to avert future water wars, and to recognize water as a basic human right to be embraced by all.

About 70 percent of the earth's surface is covered with water, but 97 percent of this water is salt water. Salt water includes not only salt but a plethora of other minerals, rendering it unsuitable for many of the purposes that human beings use water. Two percent of the water on earth is locked in glaciers in the areas of the North and South Poles; less than 1 percent of the world's water is accessible for human use.[10] If the entire world's water were fit into a gallon jug, the fresh water available for us to use would equal only about one tablespoon. It has been estimated that in fifteen years, 1.8 billion people will live in regions of severe water scarcity. As the writer Barbara Kingsolver notes, "Water is life. It's the briny broth of our origins, the pounding circulatory system of the world. We stake our civilizations on the coasts and mighty rivers. Our deepest dread is the threat of having too little—or too much."[11]

Overabundance and scarcity both threaten life. As I walked among the poorest of the poor in neighborhoods in Mumbai and Kolkata, my first impression was that water was overwhelming us; it was literally everywhere. We visited India during monsoon season, and the rain was constant. Streets flooded in no time. I found myself constantly stepping into standing water, whether I tried to avoid it or not. Massive flooding created the conditions for contaminated water. In a country where many go thirsty, too much water can be just as deadly.

Refugees who choose to face the perils of the sea understand the danger of having abundant undrinkable water, as seen by the story of fourteen Haitians who embarked on a raft for Florida. On the second day, the wind failed, stranding them under a torrid sun for three days. The heat and thirst pushed Doris over the edge. She jumped into the ocean and started to gulp the salty water, becoming thirstier with each swallow. Her friends forced her back onto the raft, but to no avail. Within an hour she was dead.

We human beings must always remain constantly close to fresh water. It literally sustains our existence. Gaining even limited access to this life-sustaining treasure can be an all-consuming task for millions of families each day. Women in developing countries (often children, too, but rarely men) walk an average of 3.7 miles to get water from boreholes, wells, and fresh streams.[12] Some women spend up to 60 percent of their day hauling water. Women and children across the globe are estimated to spend a staggering 200 million hours a day seeking water.[13] Comprehending the massive consequences of this kind of hard labor is almost impossible. Many of the jerry cans they carry can weigh forty or more pounds; the burden on their bodies is extreme. If their access to safe, clean water were secured without requiring them to carry it themselves, there would be 200 million hours available to them to be in school, to nurture their young, to engage in income-generating projects benefitting their families. Our whole world, as well as their personal futures, would look strikingly different.

The United Nations declared 2005–2015 to be the "Water for Life" decade. The goal is, by 2015, to reduce by half the proportion of people without access to safe drinking water by 2015 and to stop unsustainable exploitation of water resources. Governments pledged to this goal when they adopted the Millennium Development Goals in 2000.[14] The safe drinking water crisis is worldwide; in many urban centers like Mumbai and Kolkata, residents of shantytowns and slums remain vulnerable to waterborne diseases. The water they use flows from nearby factories and drains into sewers, usually without being treated. Slum dwellers who are officially authorized to access this water are locally termed as *bastis*. A large number of squatter settlements are not so authorized. These squatter settlements are situated along canals, large drains, garbage dumps, railway tracks, and roadsides—settlements unfit for human habitation. They consist of clusters of huts comprising several rooms constructed with temporary building materials such as polythene or tarps. Each room is occupied by a family sharing a common latrine, without proper arrangements for water supply points, drains, or disposal of solid wastes and garbage within the slum boundaries.

As a result of uncontrolled floods and poor sanitation, bacteria and other waterborne agents have threatened rural and urban populations. These residents face water shortages or receive the dregs of the formal municipal network, often making their own informal arrangements using untreated surface water and shallow tube-wells to harvest rainwater. The inadequate supply of water by the city authorities has also aggravated the problem of piped water quality. Contamination occurs when water pressures are low. When the flow ceases, a vacuum is created in the pipes, sucking in pollutants through cracks. Sewage and garbage thus enter the pipelines, and treated surface water becomes contaminated. This water can cause outbreaks of hepatitis, dysentery, and gastroenteritis during the hot and monsoon seasons.

India is also the world's tuberculosis (TB) capital. TB is a disease of poverty, striking disproportionately the already weak and malnourished. According to the World Health Organization (WHO), India has the world's largest tuberculosis epidemic.

Approximately 2 to 3 million Indian citizens are infected with TB. When I returned home to the United States from India and Africa with health issues, my doctor's first suspicion was that I may have contracted TB. The extremely poor do not have the option of returning to a healthy living environment.

The water and sanitation crisis in India reveals in graphic fashion the kind of crushing inequality harming the whole human family. Without access to healthy water sources and safe sanitation for all who inhabit our fragile planet, little hope exists for healthy living. These requirements of water and sanitation are currently found wanting in many precarious environments where the poorest of us are forced to live. People squatting in teeming slums, congestion in the streets, encroachment on public spaces, water and air pollution, and deteriorating infrastructure in major cities in developing economies have resulted from a massive increase in the world population. Inhuman living conditions still abound everywhere in our world, conditions to which only those in abject poverty, without options, are consigned. They are left struggling in places that, instead of becoming a home, are breeding grounds for disease and despair.

The story of water access in varying regions of the world remains a story of vast disparity. In places such as North Africa and the Middle East, where water is scarce, access to clean drinking water is a major factor in economic development. Most municipal reservoirs are inadequate, and their water supplies are distributed for only a few hours a day. Consumers have to store the water supplied to them in jugs, pots, or other containers. Although this is wasteful, far more water is lost through leaks in distribution lines and street taps. Corruption makes responding to the problem of scarcity more difficult.

Meanwhile, swimming pools in the United States lose 150 billion gallons of water to evaporation every year, while many in the developing world subsist on fewer than 5 gallons of water daily.[15] I have lived in North America and Europe most of my life. I have never entered a home on either continent in which water was not directly piped into the home from a secure source. The global story includes the fact that 46 percent of households across our planet do not have water piped to them. People in the United States use five times the amount of water that Europeans use, and they use about 100 gallons of water at home each day, while millions of the poorest subsist on fewer than 5 gallons.[16]

The most powerful images of the presence of water that I have seen are pictures taken from space. The space shuttle *Columbia* took photographic images of the African continent that highlights the Nile River's flow 4,180 miles northward from Jinja, Uganda, through Sudan and up into Egypt, all the way to the Mediterranean Sea. In an arresting image, one sees verdant life on the land near the Nile, while much of the areas at a farther distance from the great river become ever more barren. Most major water sources like the Nile River flow across multiple national boundaries. This leads inevitably to dialogue or even conflict over how to divvy up the water, especially when more is needed than is available. Ethiopia and Egypt continue today to be in conflict over the Nile. Uganda, Ethiopia, Kenya, Tanzania, Rwanda, Burundi, and Democratic Republic of Congo are also all dependent on the Nile River's vast but limited resources. Each nation has reason to fear when another makes increased demands on the Nile's water. In our day, Turkey and Syria continue to quarrel over the Euphrates, India and Pakistan squabble over the Indus River, and Israel and its Arab neighbors have fought over the Jordan River and its tributaries on occasions more numerous than any other river has been disputed in modern times.

I recently learned the etymology of the word "rival." It stunned me, reminding me of the centrality of water in the human drama from our very beginnings. The word derives from the Latin word *rivalis,* and it describes a competitor for a river or stream. We are no strangers to fights over water rights, which are a huge part of the human story from the very beginning. Our need for water is a powerful metaphor for humanity's common dependence upon the goods of creation. In ancient times, our forbears built thriving civilizations alongside oceans, lakes, and rivers. Wherever water was bountiful, we human beings discovered a home. In the twenty-first century, it is still striking how many of humanity's megalopolises rest on harbors of water where commerce readily flourishes and a water source is secured.

Drought and famine beleaguered the Israelites in the days of Abraham, Isaac, and Jacob's son Joseph. The eleventh of twelve sons, Joseph was unquestionably the beloved of his father and gifted with a strong will to succeed. Jealousy drove his brothers to one day sell him into slavery in Egypt. Joseph's ingenuity and resourcefulness, coupled with good fortune, led to his rise to a position of prominence while in exile. After leading Egypt through one of its most dire famines, he found it in his heart to forgive past wrongs and to shower upon his family the food security he had achieved for his new companions and for himself.

This same region of the world that experienced this legendary sibling rivalry is once again undergoing a serious drought and is witness to major national rivalries over water. Israel's meteorological department declared 2010 the hottest year since records have been kept. Palestinians lack the water needed for their families and for crop irrigation. Historical tensions and deep-rooted jealousies have endured for decades. Too severe a limit on water access for either side could result in a war sparked by disputed water rights. According to a 2009 World Bank report, Israelis use four times as much water per capita as Palestinians. Israelis admit to having greater access to water than their Palestinian counterparts, but they also attribute much of that to being more imaginative in their ways of conserving water. As is true elsewhere, much of the water is used for the agriculture necessary for growing crops, in this case to feed more than 7 million Israelis. Under Israeli military rule, West Bank Palestinians have been prevented from digging wells that allow them to access the fresh water in aquifers deep below them. Their water access is reduced solely to shallow wells, natural springs, and the rain water that evaporates quickly in the arid climate.

Thousands of miles away, to feed its rapidly accelerating demand for new energy sources, China is building a hydropower dam called the Zangmu on Tibet's Yarlung Tsangpo River, which flows into India and Pakistan as the Brahmaputra River. China may eventually build as many as sixty dams on the Tibetan

Plateau. Tibet's neighbors fear it will disrupt their access to a safe and stable water supply.[17] These battles are taking place in the developed world, too. For example, in the United States, the Colorado River has been a battleground for decades between a number of thirsty western states, and now the Red River is a source of contention in a number of the arid states it serves, principally Texas, Oklahoma, Arkansas, and Louisiana.[18] At the heart of the divisive issue, Texas claims it is entitled to billions of gallons of water from the Oklahoma side of the river basin. Oklahoma counters that Texas is not doing enough to conserve. The US Supreme Court has been called upon to settle the issue.

Although water disputes can cause intractable conflict between cultures, water has a symbolic and even sacred status in nearly every world religion. It cleanses the body, and by extension purifies both body and spirit. In India, the water of the river Ganga (also known as the Ganges) is treated with a special reverence. In Nashik, the Godavari River, which connects to the Ganga, is a place where pilgrims flock every year. Hundreds of thousands of faithful come here to have their sins washed away. They immerse themselves in the flowing water, establishing a divine sense of togetherness with their fellow worshipers. This river is also considered to be a loving mother, dispensing bounty, fertility, and prosperity to the faithful. The greatest water channel in India, it is also considered its most sacred. Millions of Hindus call it Mother Ganges. Each year millions of people visit it, bathe in it, and take samples of water home. The sick and the poor hope to be cured by the water or to see their economic status improve. If they are not cured, then they at least hope to die in its comforting and holy waters.

Temples throughout India represent and honor different gods. Hindus go to the temple to worship as individuals. They do not worship as a congregation, nor is there any day set aside for worship. The temples can be spread over acres and are like little towns. In the outer areas one finds tanks for ritualistic bathing, shrines, halls, and bazaars. Artists and sculptors practice their professions and sell their wares. Vendors sell flowers, sandalwood, and souvenirs. The inner part of the temple is where the image of the goddess is kept. As one prays in this cool, darkened prayer hall, the soul is believed to unite with the three forms of the creator (Brahman). Religious Hindus also start their mornings with personal prayer and religious rituals (*puja*). The worship should not begin until one visits a stream to touch the purifying waters. And even though India is a nation historically with a social stratification system, when it comes to ritual performances, all are united. For instance, during the holy bath, both the rich and the poor are seen in the same river, since their gods treats everyone equally.

Regrettably, millions of young people face uncertain futures, placed in jeopardy by happenstance: the place they were born. Of the approximately 60 million newborns entering the human family in our towns and cities, these children will more likely grow up in a slum, in the informal settlements that sprout up in megacities, or in temporary, makeshift housing, all of which lack clean water and sanitation. Such cramped and unhealthy living arrangements offer fertile ground for diseases like TB. Every fifteen seconds a child dies somewhere in our fragile world because of a water-related illness; lack of access to clean water and sanitation kills our children at a rate equivalent to a jumbo jet crashing every four hours. Nearly all these deaths occur in the developing world. Far too few of us across the globe sense the full impact of this colossal defeat for humanity. I am struck by the fact that, in my lifetime, the global water and sanitation crisis has claimed more lives through disease than all the wars we have waged—a fact that fails to capture our attention or enter our history books.

Greater human ingenuity has a vital, indispensable role to play in the fashioning of safer, more humane communities possessing clean water and sanitation. What I witnessed in the streets of Mumbai and Kolkata, and what billions of people witness and endure every day, is a crisis that requires ingenuity if we are to find solutions or ameliorate human suffering. But ingenuity can take us only so far. Equally important is the way we look upon each other. I have come to believe that, to the extent that we foster new and creative ways of perceiving and protecting the invisible ties that bind us, we can transform humanity's defeats into the long-awaited day when we save all our children from preventable deaths.

Notes

[1] Charles Bukowski, *The Captain Is Out to Lunch and the Sailors Have Taken Over the Ship* (New York: HarperCollins, 2004), 10.

[2] Fyodor Dostoevsky, *The Idiot*, trans. David McDuff (Penguin, Amazon Digital Services), 72.

[3] Ibid.

[4] Michel de Montaigne, "Of Custom," *1575 Essays*, trans. Charles Cotton, http://oregonstate.edu/instruct/phl302/texts/montaigne/m-essays_contents.html.

[5] Jorge Luis Borges, "Funes, His Memory," in *Collected Fictions*, trans. Andrew Hurley (New York: Penguin, 1998), 135.

[6] Ibid., 137.

[7] Katherine Boo, *Behind the Beautiful Forevers* (New York: Random House, 2012).

[8] René Descartes, *Discourse on Method and Meditations on First Philosophy*, trans. Donald Cress, 4th ed. (Indianapolis: Hackett, 1998), 4.

[9] See especially Epicurus's "Letter to Menoeceus," http://classics.mit.edu/Epicurus/menoec.html.

[10] Fairfax Water, "The Story of Drinking Water," http://www.fcwa.org/story_of_water/html/earth.htm.

[11] Barbara Kingsolver as quoted in *National Geographic*, "A Special Issue: Water Our Thirsty World," April 2010, 38. Hereafter cited as *NG*.

[12] Ibid.

[13] Ibid.

[14] Ibid.

[15] See http://www.globalcitizencorps.org/groups/issue-water/15734.

[16] *NG*, 150.

[17] Richard Finney, "Concerns Arise over China's Dam Building Drive in Tibet," Radio Free Asia, April 17, 2013.

[18] Sadhbh Walshe, "Red River Water Wars: Four States Battle over Water Access," *The Guardian*, May 9, 2013.

Chapter 5

What (in the World) Is to Be Done?

We must not see *any* person as an abstraction. Instead, we must see in every person a universe with its own secrets, with its own treasures, with its own sources of anguish, and with some measure of triumph.

—*Elie Wiesel*[1]

Jim

In the previous chapter we saw the promise that personal experience holds for broadening one's horizons and understanding the challenges facing so many in the world today. But we also saw that personal experience is not a foolproof solution to the challenges posed by appeals to logic and emotion. In fact, personal experience seems to have just as many limitations. Arguments can be logically convincing but practically unpersuasive. Empathetic appeals can motivate action, but they can also result in a false and even manipulative form of solidarity. Personal experience seems to combine the best elements of the first two strategies: it motivates action *and* provides a check on manipulation, since those taking action have personally witnessed the situation they are trying to remedy. But, sadly, we are all too easily blinded by the force of habit, unable to sustain the intensity of the meaningful experiences we do have. Even when memory is not fleeting, it is still subject to shifting (and sometimes conflicting) interpretations, and drawing general conclusions from unique personal experiences is difficult. If solidarity is the appropriate moral goal, how can these dilemmas be resolved? The first step toward cultivating an authentic ethic of solidarity is to beware of false idols. The idea of a "universal humanity" is a high-minded but meaningless phrase unless given some specific content. In other words, all our obligations are, in a sense, particular. There is no universal human, but only difficult decisions about which seemingly intractable problems we should invest our time and money to mitigate. The sad irony is that someone unwilling to do the hard work of determining what the common good really means is more likely to be narcissistic without even knowing it. Consider, for instance, a nongovernmental organization (NGO) with the primary aim of promoting fair-trade coffee without ever truly paying attention to the actual conditions of specific coffee farmers. The NGO knows it is working for a good cause in the abstract, but it also presumes that it understands the plight of the farmers. Then it backs up this false belief with well-intentioned but vacuous cosmopolitan rhetoric.

Another example comes from a fascinating account of life in Mumbai, written by Father Placido Fonseca. This self-published book is called *Tracks*, and the title is meant to evoke, among other connections, the train tracks that lead poor children to the supposed big-city promised land. Unsurprisingly, these children are gravely disappointed when they arrive, and they have to find some way to fend for themselves. Father Placie, as he is known, is the director of an organization called Snehasadan, and he welcomes these children into a number of private (but Snehasadan-sponsored) homes with open arms. We met him in his office in Mumbai, and he thoughtfully gave us copies of his book. It is a treasure trove of insightful observations about solidarity and caring for others. He raises an ironic observation about the ways in which NGOs in Mumbai mishandle the dilemma of "street children": "Today, a lone child getting off a train in a bustling station like CST [in Mumbai] will be met with at least eight to ten organizations who work for children. What would have worked for the benefit of the child, however, might upset and alienate the child further as most often, these organizations will fight with each other for rights over this child, to be able to take him or her into their institutions."² In their well-intentioned rush to protect children from exploitation, these organizations often neglect to coordinate their efforts. Sometimes they may even need to bolster their own numbers so that they can report their success to donors.

It is tempting, and easier than ever, to claim the moral high ground by pursuing what we think is the common good. The vast amount of information available nowadays makes it natural for us to think that we know more than we actually do. This became clear in the earlier discussion of slacktivism: watching the Kony 2012 video, for example, might lead me to believe that I understand this complex problem. The false form of solidarity thrives in a world where information is widely available but often superficial, trivial, or even misleading. It goes hand in hand with a culture of narcissism that substitutes the individual will for genuine social interactions. Actually interacting with other people often challenges our prepackaged views of the world, while gathering information online, even from a variety of sources, tempts us to select what we want to believe based on our own preferences. For instance, does webmd.com empower us to make decisions about our health, or does the overwhelming amount of information and the near-infinite number of possible diagnoses lead to confusion and error?

In May 2012 *The Atlantic* published an article arguing that social media has the ironic effect of making us more alienated and alone.³ Even if it has the potential to unite people, the kind of connections it makes possible might be so tenuous as to further isolate individuals. These individuals might believe that they have connected with others on some level, yet they feel more alone than ever. Social networks become vehicles for self-indulgent status updates whose sole purpose is to be liked by as many friends as possible.

My favorite expression of another version of this self-deceived and narcissistic form of solidarity is a story published by *The Onion*, a humorous online and print magazine that publishes fake news stories. In a story titled "Semester Abroad Spent

Drinking with Other American Students," the writers parody
the common study-abroad experience of wanting to experience
a new culture but really only experiencing what is already familiar.[4] The students conclude that it is indeed a "small world," after
they meet and hang out exclusively with other students from
neighboring colleges who are also studying abroad. They praise
the international character of Seville, explaining that, because
of this fact, they do not need to learn Spanish. Perhaps when
these same students return home with their initial perspective
unchallenged and unchanged, they will blog about their authentic experience. Perhaps their friends will confirm their status as
intercultural explorers.

In a 2007 article in *America* magazine, John Kavanaugh
expresses a deep concern about this culture of narcissism, even
suggesting that it has roots in the American obsession with
autonomous individualism. To be autonomous is to be self-ruling, but Kavanaugh worries that this attitude can "degenerate
into a conviction that there is no rule higher than one's self and
that there is no other source than oneself to consult."[5] He points
out that individuals are not self-made, so they are never autonomous in the most literal sense. Not only is it senseless to regard
oneself as completely self-ruling, but it is also dangerous, under-
cutting the pursuit of the common good. He concludes, "Now,
perhaps more than ever, it is time to reaffirm the tradition of the
common good in our moral and political life. But this will not
occur if the only trump cards we hold are called individualism
and autonomy."[6]

Kavanaugh is right to be concerned about a culture that promotes the will of the individual at all costs, but he is wrong about
the relationship between individual autonomy and the common
good. As we have already seen, it is just as easy to be narcissistic
in the pursuit of a false form of solidarity as it is to be narcissistic in the pursuit of autonomy. And he ends up affirming
the same stereotypical definition of autonomy that he criticizes:
"For autonomous individualism, there is no objective truth or
value before which one's will, one's liberty, must yield in obedi-
ence."[7] This simply is not true: Immanuel Kant, perhaps the most

famous proponent of this concept in the history of moral philosophy, flatly rejects the idea that autonomy simply means doing what you will. It is not hard to see why this definition fails, for if you always did just what you willed at the time, you would be a slave to impulse.

For instance, acting on a desire to eat all the food in my refrigerator does not make me autonomous. On the contrary, it means that I have failed to recognize the objective truth that eating all that food is actually bad for my health. True autonomy is subject to all sorts of constraints. For Kant, my will must be constrained by respect for the moral law. Likewise, the will of the glutton must be constrained by a standard of health that he obviously doesn't invent for himself. Otherwise, he is a slave. His true autonomy is derived not from doing whatever he wants but from having the ability to impose limits on his will. This, of course, assumes that he has the freedom to make such a choice. In other words, you can choose to fast if you decide to forgo food you have access to; the person who has no food cannot be said to starve autonomously.

It is too easy to denigrate the idea of autonomous individualism while defending the idea of the common good. Both concepts are complicated, and autonomous individualism has probably advanced the cosmopolitan cause as much or more than the idea of the common good. Take, for instance, the international impact of the idea of universal human rights within the past century. While this idea is in a sense grounded in the idea of a universal humanity, it is more clearly dependent upon the fundamental and unique value of each individual. Kavanaugh's own defense of Catholic social justice might be more clearly derived from the belief that each individual is made in the image and likeness of God, focusing on the individual rather than some vague sense of the common good.

Consider the profound impact of Amartya Sen's "capabilities approach" on questions of welfare economics.[8] Sen has persuasively argued that poverty must be understood not simply in general terms (i.e., a country's gross domestic product), but more importantly in the way it prevents individuals from making free and autonomous decisions. He highlights the moral dimension of poverty by focusing on its impact on individuals who are harmed by persistent and structural inequalities. Although Kavanaugh is right to point out the myth of the self-made individual, he fails to consider the fact that some individuals are more self-made than others as a direct result of economic conditions. Sen has shown this to be both an economic fact and a moral tragedy.

Simply having more options does not mean that I have more freedom. Sometimes, in fact, it can be an impediment to free choice. If I have to choose between one hundred different types of cereal, I might end up putting the first box I see (or the one with the best packaging, or the one with the catchiest character) in my cart. In this case, I have not exercised my freedom, since I have chosen arbitrarily. In fact, it would be hard to make an informed and free choice given these conditions. Maybe that is why advertising is such big business: in a land of overwhelming choices, something has to nudge me from my cereal-aisle stupor. But if I live under conditions that offer no meaningful choices, it makes sense to say that I cannot determine my own fate. I am subject to external constraints not of my making that determine the kinds of choices I can make. So, although having more options does not make us more self-made, having some meaningful choice seems crucial. In *Behind the Beautiful Forevers*, Abdul's father, Karam Husain, makes this precise point: "Everybody in Annawadi talks like this—oh, I will make my child a doctor, a lawyer, and he will make us rich. It's vanity, nothing more. Your little boat goes west and you congratulate yourself, 'What a navigator I am!' And then the wind blows you east."[9] Another influential perspective on Catholic social justice is the "preferential option for the poor."[10] This view insists that Christians have a gospel duty to give the poor special priority in questions of economic justice. On one hand, it makes sense to claim that a historically oppressed group should have their perspective validated instead of marginalized. But again, the preferential option for the poor can be misinterpreted, and the unintended result can lead to further dehumanization of the poor. Presenting the plight of "street children" might motivate people to act on their behalf, but, as Father Placie cautions us, this label also "puts a child in a slot and experience shows that even after years off the street, it is difficult to rid oneself of the habit and culture associated with labeling."[11] The preferential option for the poor is good only insofar as it actually enhances the ability of those individuals to live meaningful lives. When misinterpreted, it becomes just another weapon against them, just another form of dehumanization. Poverty becomes an essential feature of their humanity instead of a complicated and variable feature of their circumstances.

After we accomplish the first step of avoiding false cosmopolitan idols, we must next learn to live with two competing truths: (1) whether by fortune or fate, there are profound differences between individuals that impact their abilities to determine the course of their own lives; and (2) these differences, however morally arbitrary they are, can only be mitigated and never overcome.

One way of explaining these two truths is through the following example. Every year, my friends and I have a college roommate reunion. This typically involves lots of food and a variety of board games, the best of which is called *Settlers of Catan*. The premise of the game is to colonize territories rich in resources (ore, timber, brick, sheep, and wheat). The right combination of resources enables the player to build cities, roads, armies, and so forth. Markers are placed on each territory to represent possible dice combinations (e.g., you could own an ore with a 3 on it or a wheat with an 8 on it). Resources are collected when the dice are rolled and the number shown matches the number on the territory. The person who reaches a certain number of development points first wins the game.

Two features of this game offer some insight into the two competing truths just mentioned. First, one of the territories on the board is a desert: there are no resources here, and the placement of the desert hugely influences how desirable other adjacent territories are. The initial placement of the territories is completely random, which can drastically alter the game. Second, the placement of the markers is also random, so your strategy is often entirely dependent on the probability that the number will be rolled. For instance, I might start with a strategy that requires me to collect ore, but seeing that an 8 is much more likely to be rolled than a 3, I might switch to a strategy that calls for me to collect wheat instead.

This game helps us to appreciate just how much is left up to luck; it would be a very different game were the board to be arranged otherwise and the markers to be shifted just a little. The real-life version of this is the vast difference in resources that have been both blessings and curses for their countries. Suppose Saudi Arabia didn't have any oil. Suppose Rwanda did. How different would the world look? For many years, the United States enjoyed a kind of geopolitical isolation that wouldn't have been possible if we had been closer in proximity to Europe. However, we discovered on December 7, 1941, that Hawaii was not far enough from Japan.

A fascinating show on the History Channel called *How the States Got Their Shapes* makes this exact point. Even the boundaries of our own states were established based on a combination of total accident and political compromise. Perhaps the clearest example is the idea of gerrymandering in politics: when one party gains power, it immediately seeks to redraw district maps to increase its chances of staying in power. The boundaries that divide us, then, are surprisingly accidental.

On the other hand, the game reminds us that despite the fact that everything could have been otherwise, in real life this is the only "game" we have. On our reunion weekends, we can simply dismantle the board once someone wins. In real life, however, the roots of what strikes us as contingent and even arbitrary have grown so deep that they cannot simply be dug up. For instance, when critics claim that Israel is an "invented state," they might mean two very different things: either that Israel as a people with an ancient claim is a myth, or that Israel as a nation with borders is a recent invention. The second meaning is undoubtedly true (since Israel as a nation with borders did not exist prior to 1948), but also uninteresting. Every state is similarly invented. Yet this observation does not make these states, or the conflicts between them, any less real.

The *Settlers of Catan* example may seem trivial, but I think that its lesson is profound. A false form of solidarity promotes the idea that all would be right in the world if we could simply separate reality from illusion, the necessary from the contingent, the wheat from the chaff. If we could see that so many of the differences between individuals and between countries are completely morally arbitrary, then we could embrace a cosmopolitan ethic that unites instead of divides. Perhaps the reason that these pleas have had logical but not practical force, and why they often smack of emotional manipulation, is that they are only half-right. Asking whether I am my brother's keeper is different from insisting that I am my brother. Some individual differences are as absolutely real as they are completely accidental.

On a Travel Channel show called *Bizarre Foods*, the host, Andrew Zimmern, constantly preaches to his viewers and to his hosts about the power that food has to unite people from different cultures. I find this idea appealing, and I even cofounded a Multicultural Culinary Society in college. Our organization was short-lived, but we did host a benefit dinner for poverty relief in Kenya that combined Kenyan food with guest lectures about the country. To his credit, Zimmern seems honest when asked whether he likes a particular dish, often deciding not to take a second bite. Yet there are times when the preaching of cross-cultural bonds wears thin.

In one episode, Zimmern visited Uganda and took part in a spirit possession ceremony. He confides to his viewers that, though he is acting like everyone else, he is not really channeling spirits. It is not clear what this claim even means: he is not a member of that tribe, nor does he share any of their cultural and religious views. It is unnecessary to point out the obvious fact that he is not actually channeling spirits. His tone suggests that he finds the whole idea to be quaint. Whether it is his failure or the ceremony's, the implication is that he could have possibly experienced this culture in an authentic way. Such an idea seems totally wrongheaded and strange. It would have been an excellent time to remind viewers that traveling exposes fundamental differences in belief systems and values, just as it can also lead to cross-cultural understanding. Yet Zimmern fails to take advantage of this opportunity, choosing instead to add a voiceover commentary after the scene was filmed to explain his play-acting. He continues to preach solidarity between cultures to his hosts, even after letting his viewers in on the secret.

Imagine the outcry in the Catholic community if Zimmern were to attend Mass and pretend to be moved by the Holy Spirit. He would add a voiceover (after the fact) explaining that he was simply playing along and mimicking the actions of the religious faithful. Wouldn't the Catholic critic claim that he had misunderstood what is possible for someone with no experience in that tradition?

The real challenge, then, is to determine which of these accidental differences are absolutely real and necessary, and which lead to unjust social arrangements that can be remedied through political action. In other words, although Zimmern was foolish to imply that the spirit possession could have worked (whatever that means), it might still be true that Americans have some obligations to the tribe Zimmern visited. True cosmopolitanism overcomes parochial bias and narrow self-interest, but it refuses to dismiss every cultural difference as a mere illusion.

In the American philosophical tradition, John Rawls provides us with a strategy inspired by Immanuel Kant for determining which differences are arbitrary from a moral point of view.[12] Rawls points out that, in order to determine the principles of a just society, we cannot simply ask people what they think. We are hopelessly blinded by our own self-interest in ways we might not even recognize. If I am rich, and you ask me whether I think health care is a right that should be universal, I am more likely to say no than yes. While I might have excellent reasons for thinking this way, it might also be true that I am biased by my own wealth and my desire not to subsidize health care for others. On the other hand, if I cannot afford health care and you ask me whether it is a right, I am probably going to say yes. Again, I might have good reasons for saying this. Still, my self-interest no doubt strongly influences my view. Rawls's point, then, is that we have to find a way to think impartially about these hard questions.

Rawls takes his argument one step further before providing his solution. He points out that many of the facts about ourselves that cause this bias were not even truly up to us. For instance, neither the person born rich nor the person born poor did this for themselves. It happened to them, much like winning or losing the lottery. Even wealth acquired through hard work does not seem absolutely my own doing, since basic character traits like ambition, not to mention the opportunity to excel, are not entirely up to me. Wherever ambition comes from, it seems clear that being raised in a nurturing household cultivates it. His point is that we are not self-made: by the accidents of nature or nurture, we have had the good (or not so good) fortune of becoming who we are.

But how can we determine what a just society would look like when so many of the factors that make it up were simply a matter of luck? Rawls proposes a thought experiment called "the veil of ignorance" to solve this problem. If we want to know what obligations we have to others, we must remain ignorant of all of the contingent facts about ourselves. That is, we must ignore the facts about ourselves that were not up to us. Race, gender, economic status, and even (perhaps most controversially) ambition are examples of such facts. For example, I did not choose my race or gender, and my ambition is at least heavily influenced, if not determined, by the way I was raised and the opportunities I have been afforded.

The question, then, is what scheme of rights and obligations would I agree to if I did not know what role I occupied in society? Rawls's thought experiment serves as justification for the redistribution of wealth, since this type of inequality results in a deep way from morally contingent factors. This does not mean, however, that everyone deserves the same amount of material goods. Some forms of inequality can be justified by proving beneficial even to the least well off. A society that gives its citizens financial incentives to study brain surgery (compensating them for their time and talent) is better off than one that pays everyone equally regardless of what they do. Still, a substantial redistribution of wealth is justified in Rawls's view.

But, so the cosmopolitan argues, my national identity is just as much a contingent fact about me as my race and gender. I happened to be born into a particular society, be it wealthy or struggling. So perhaps it would be wrong, and merely prejudicial, to assume that my obligations stop at my nation's borders. I would be drawing a line that is completely arbitrary from a moral point of view. As Peter Singer reminds us, geography is not a morally relevant fact and hunger is hunger wherever it is found.

Robert Nozick, Rawls's determined critic, poses a thought experiment of his own to challenge the idea of a veil of ignorance. If many qualities we deem to be central to our identity are also (from a moral perspective) contingent facts about us, how far can we take this line of argument? After all, people born blind do not deserve that either, and no one who can see gave themselves this gift. If blindness and sightedness are also contingent facts about us, then why not redistribute retinas to eradicate this inequality?[13] Of course, Nozick is just joking at this point; he does not actually think we should redistribute retinas. But he uses this extreme example to ask why the redistribution of wealth is different in principle? The money that I earn is not as much a part of me as my retinas, but they are equally contingent facts about me from a moral perspective. By taking Rawls's logic to the extreme, Nozick forces us to ask what can properly be claimed as mine, and what I owe to my fellow citizens. Singer might add that we should not stop at our fellow citizens, but that our moral obligation extends equally to those in other countries, especially the least well off.

Here, as in the *Settlers of Catan* example, we see that two competing truths—something can be both morally arbitrary and very real—cannot be reconciled, but they can still both be true. In a quote originally attributed to the football coach Barry Switzer (and made popular by the former governor of Texas Ann Richards), "Some people are born on third base and go through life thinking they hit a triple." The only thing this adage gets wrong is the way it limits itself to "some people." We are, perhaps in our very nature, quick to claim responsibility for what is deeply dependent on divine plan, fortune, or fate. This is especially true when the outcome is favorable for us; we are much quicker to blame our faults on accidents of nature and nurture. Rawls is right to point out that people confuse their good fortune with something they have accomplished on their own. But Nozick would counter by saying that we need some way of determining what people are permitted to claim as their own (despite this element of luck). The fact that we deceive ourselves into believing that we "hit a triple" does not negate the fact that some of us are, in fact, on "third base."

Once we have forsworn false idols and realized this second point, we can move on to the third step. As we discussed earlier, the idea of solidarity implies that we are raising consciousness and not just cash. In other words, it would be wrong to think of solidarity as a simple transfer of wealth from the rich to the poor. Although solidarity refers to one's *actions*, it refers just as much to one's *beliefs*. Consider, for example, a prominent white businessman who donates $1 million to the United Negro College Fund (UNCF). Privately this man may have many different reasons for doing this. Maybe he genuinely cares about educating young African Americans; maybe he pities them and hopes that more money will solve the problem; maybe he is a racist who knows that the donation will give him excellent publicity and might even provide cover for his own personal biases. Even though the UNCF gets the same amount of money regardless, only one of these attitudes seems like a form of true solidarity.

In rare but interesting cases, one might have to choose between transferring wealth and genuinely interacting with people in other cultures. On our first trip to Uganda in 2001 I negotiated a price for a *batik* (a decorative wall hanging). While foreign to most people in the United States, negotiating is widespread throughout much of the world. A negotiation, especially one involving an obvious foreigner, can take quite a long time. It usually begins with a grossly inflated asking price, followed by a flat rejection (I was taught to accompany this with a high-pitched "ehhhh?!"). The seller, unfazed by the implication that her original price was insane, talks up the merits of the item and reluctantly lowers the price a little. The potential buyer starts to walk away, returning only when the seller calls him back. More numbers are exchanged, and no one is satisfied by these new figures either. Sometimes an item changes hands. The whole process can be tedious and exhausting, but it can also momentarily break down cultural borders. The conversation seems a little aggressive on its surface, but it's done with a wink and a nod. Vendors are probably disappointed that an obvious foreigner refused to overpay; part of me thinks, though, that they respect someone willing to participate in the daily battle of negotiation. On this particular occasion, I did not buy the batik. Another buyer jumped in and overpaid. It was, in fact, my uncle Don, and he immediately gave me the wall hanging. We joke about our different attitudes toward negotiating: I enjoyed doing it and sometimes felt like I was having a genuine experience of another culture. Don, on the other hand, recognized that he didn't need to negotiate and that money infused into the local economy was generally money well spent. Which one of us was in greater solidarity with the people whose goods we bought in Africa?

In his 1877 essay called "The Ethics of Belief," William Clifford defends the idea that my beliefs, and not just my actions, are morally relevant.[14] He sets up an intriguing example of a ship captain who, silencing his own doubts about whether his boat was seaworthy, let his passengers embark. In one case, all the passengers on the boat died when the captain's concerns were confirmed. In another version of the story, the ship arrives at the port unharmed, the passengers survive, and no one except the captain knows the great danger they all faced. Clifford's point is that the captain's guilt or innocence does not depend on whether the boat actually sinks. He is culpable either way. Or consider the case of drunk driver who professes his moral purity simply based on the fact that he hasn't yet killed anyone. Just because he has been fortunate thus far does not mean that getting behind the wheel drunk was less of a crime morally.

Recognizing that solidarity is about beliefs as well as actions means that it requires the cultivation of a certain kind of self-understanding; it is more accurate to say that one *becomes* rather than one *is* a citizen of the world. Consider, for instance, the

Jesuit tradition of spiritual exercises, or any number of philosophical traditions that counsel self-formation. The shared idea here
is an interest in cultivating a certain kind of self-understanding
through a daily routine of spiritual and intellectual exercises. St.
Ignatius of Loyola conceived of spiritual exercises as meditative
practice whose goal is the "conquest of self and the regulation
of one's life in such a way that no decision is made under the
influence of any inordinate attachment."[15] Recall that ancient
philosophers like the Stoics and the Epicureans pursued similar goals. Websites like "The Hunger Site" can help or hinder
this routine; they provide an opportunity for reflection, but they
might also give a false sense of having already achieved a cosmopolitan identity.

Spiritual exercise is the (not always effective) antidote to the
habits that, as Montaigne again reminds us, "put to sleep the eye
of judgment." That is, we are so anesthetized by daily routine that
we often miss opportunities to become more cosmopolitan. For
an example of the power of habit and the value of reflecting on
it, consider my difficulties driving on the highways in Atlanta.
Every morning I would get angry at inconsiderate drivers. This
makes perfect sense in Atlanta, where drivers aggressively navi-
gate superhighways. Yet, since I had the same response every day,
this anger was totally irrational. If only I could remind myself
what I would be dealing with on the highway, I might have
found a sense of peace. And my assumptions regarding the reasons that people speed might have all been wrong. Maybe they
were mothers rushing to take their children to school instead of
simply thoughtless people out to ruin my day. In a similar manner, there are probably lots of opportunities to help others that I
simply miss by being, so to speak, asleep at the wheel.

One example of a habit that often anesthetizes us is the pursuit of wealth for its own sake. In a June 2012 article in the
Chronicle of Higher Education titled "In Praise of Leisure," the authors, Robert and Edward Skidelsky, point out that we are so
conditioned by a culture of conspicuous consumption that we
have forgotten the purpose behind money. They write, "The irony, however, is that now that we have at last achieved abundance,

the habits bred into us by capitalism have left us incapable of enjoying it properly."[16] Often we work without any real sense of what the purpose of work is or should be. When we don't pose hard questions about the "good life," we end up turning the means of living well into the goal itself. But, as the authors point out, "To say that my purpose in life is to make more and more money is like saying that my aim in eating is to get fatter and fatter."[17] Although this criticism has its flaws, the authors might be right to claim that we have lost sight of the big picture. Perhaps we are habituated so that we no longer reflect on the meaning of work as a human activity.

Not having the proper perspective on our attitudes toward wealth can lead to comical moments. A friend of mine used to tell the story of attending a Bob Dylan concert at an expensive and exclusive university. Dylan, normally dour on stage, started to smile radiantly when he sang his classic hit, "Like a Rolling Stone." All the students cheered loudly. At that moment my friend realized that Dylan was smiling because he was singing to a crowd that completely missed the point of the song. The irony was overwhelming, and it probably explains Dylan's rare smile:

> Once upon a time you dressed so fine
> You threw the bums a dime in your prime, didn't you?
> People'd call, say, "Beware doll, you're bound to fall"
> You thought they were all kiddin' you
> You used to laugh about
> Everybody that was hangin' out
> Now you don't talk so loud
> Now you don't seem so proud
> About having to be scrounging for your next meal.

The students were so anesthetized by their own good fortune that they resembled the character in the song before his or her epic fall.

In a brilliant *Rolling Stone* article titled "The Fallen," Jeff Tietz spent time with several formerly prosperous families who were devastated by the financial crisis of 2008.[18] The article focuses on the psychological effects of being blindsided by this kind of unforeseeable catastrophe. The daily challenge faced by these families has as much to do with their new social status as it does with satisfying their basic needs. And yet, it is undeniable that anyone could, in principle, find him or herself in such a position. The rich are better insulted from such a radical change in their self-identity, but even this is often an illusion. In 2008, billions dried up overnight as market forces obliterated the economy.

I will never forget my irrational reaction to the news that Al Lerner, the billionaire owner of the Cleveland Browns, had died of cancer in October 2002. I could not believe that someone with so much money would actually die of a disease that can be treated, especially someone who had donated so much to the world-class hospital where he was a patient. It didn't immediately occur to me that he might not have a treatable form, nor did I consider the fact that cancer can't be bribed, even with billions. Several years later, my uncle Don told me that a small boat we had taken to get to an island in Lake Victoria in 2001 had sunk. Everyone on the boat had died, including a passenger who was reputed to be quite wealthy. When Don's Ugandan friend heard the news, she (like me when I heard about Lerner's death) couldn't believe that even the rich person drowned.

If we have forgotten the purpose of money (confusing its utility with an often unrelenting pursuit of it as an end), we are also hypnotized into thinking that our economic future (and even our identity) is stable. We seldom, if ever, are put in a position of considering how precarious our own fate really is. Being in solidarity with others is an invitation to see through such illusions, and to realize that "there but for the grace of God go I."

Those who preach cosmopolitanism as a kind of universal moral command often ignore the need for the daily spiritual and intellectual exercise that can lead to a change in self-understanding. Acquiring new habits and dispositions is a daily challenge, demanding not just action but also awareness, not just experience but meaningful reflection on that experience. It means never accepting things simply for how they are, but also never falling victim to the fancy but empty moral rhetoric that denies reality.

Becoming a citizen of the world means seeing the world from two perspectives, both of which are true even though they cannot be reconciled: day-to-day experience and meaningful reflection on those experiences.

The following story illustrates this point: A few years back, I wanted to visit a friend who had just moved to Greenville, South Carolina. I had no idea where in the state Greenville was, nor did I know how to get to his house once I arrived in the city. (The simply answer, I realize, was to have a GPS, but that is not relevant to the example!) Clearly I needed two different maps, or at least two different views of the route to his house. The first was the "view from above," in this case a view of the state map of South Carolina. The virtue of this view is that it is crystal clear, a line marking the borders of the state and a dot where Greenville is. The downfall of this view is that it lacks all the relevant detail needed to get to my friend's house. It might be clear, but it is also hopelessly abstract. The other view I needed was the "view on the ground," in this case a map of the city of Greenville that would give me directions to his house. The problem with this map is that, despite all the intricate detail, it lacks clarity. To a person unfamiliar with the city, it looks like a bunch of jumbled lines. One view is clear but not at all detailed; the other view is full of detail but is no longer clear.

Our day-to-day experience is like the second map. Experience alone does not provide us with the perspective for making sense of it, for finding meaning in it. We also need a moment of reflection (the first map) to gain some perspective on our lives. Yet we are guilty of a false form of solidarity if we think that the big picture alone can provide us with all the truth we need. We make the same mistake as Salinger's Franny, who judged everyone else based on her own supposedly enlightened and selfless philosophy. Unlike her, we must always return to the reality of day-to-day life. The moral challenge, the daily task, is to find a way to alternate between both views. We cannot see the world from both perspectives simultaneously, just like it wouldn't make sense to superimpose a city map on top of a state map.

Both perspectives have something important to contribute to our understanding of the world. Simply living life without ever reflecting on it produces a life devoid of meaning, and it makes us more likely to be morally blind to injustice that surrounds us. On the other hand, confusing the moral clarity of our reflections with the complicated and detailed business of daily life only makes us self-righteous. It does not lead to genuine understanding or to an actual change in our practices. It would be like trying to determine the degree of responsibility in a complicated manslaughter trial by repeating the commandment "Thou shall not kill" over and over. Even if we can all agree that killing is wrong, the messy business of real life resists our attempts to impose crystal-clear rules on it.

The same challenge confronts us when we attempt to cultivate an authentic moral imagination. On one hand, an imagination that is too utopian forgets, as the old saying goes, that the perfect is the enemy of the good. Progress is always made incrementally, in fits and starts. Aside from being unrealistic, a utopian imagination runs the risk of becoming smug and self-satisfied. On the other hand, we can become so entrenched in the gritty details of moral and political progress that they overwhelm us. We risk becoming cynical about our capacity to effect change, forgetting the importance of imagined future possibilities. Unless there is a future-oriented, though not utopian, element to our moral imagination, we will never even conceive of the goals we wish to pursue. We need both views of human experience: the view from above and the view on the ground.

Unfortunately, although both of these perspectives are necessary, we cannot see our lives from both perspectives at the same time. We either get caught up in the day-to-day details of our lives, or we reflect on the big-picture significance of these events. Our inability to have both views in mind at once might be regarded as a kind of original sin. At the very least, it means that we lack the omniscience required to practice infallibly an ethic of solidarity. Our moral imagination seems seriously limited, not just because we are prone to hypocrisy, but also because of our very nature.

One example of this can be found in a quote attributed to the infamous Josef Stalin: "One death is a tragedy; one million is a statistic." The human mind and heart do not seem capable of processing all the pain in the world. Even the attempt to do so is often circumvented by the easier and happier activity of diverting our attention away from this suffering. We become absorbed in daily tasks that hold our moral imagination hostage. And when we find ourselves concerned, even outraged, it is more likely to be about some small offense than about fundamental injustice in the world. In a defiant contrast to Stalin's claim, the Holocaust survivor Abel Herzberg has remarked, "There were not 6 million Jews murdered; there was one murder, 6 million times."[19] This echoes the view expressed by Elie Wiesel in the quote that introduced this chapter. But do Herzberg and Wiesel ask us to do the morally impossible? How can we avoid seeing individuals as (to use Wiesel's term) abstractions, when our day-to-day lives are guided by the sedative effect of habit? They seem to be asking us to stare into the sun of moral truth, but whether this can be sustained is the real question.

If we are unable to see each individual as a universe unto him or herself, then our very nature seems resistant to the idea of being a citizen of the world. It seems that we are prone to the original sin of moral blindness. Even if we can glimpse the righteous truth of cosmopolitanism from time to time, we can only ever mitigate, rather than eliminate, the inequality that results from the differences between individuals. For what, then, are we responsible? What is up to us, and what lies outside the limits of human control?

Don

I am sitting on the veranda of a small, lovely new home in Gulu, northern Uganda. This home is drawing the curiosity of scores of people from all across this region of the world. Why? This new house is made principally from what other people discard. Indeed, there are ten thousand water bottles, bottles that were emptied and then simply discarded, that are now forming the walls of this new structure. They were filled with ordinary soil and encased with cement on the outside. Throngs of people come here every week to see something altogether original: a water bottle house. I feel honored to be the first houseguest in this extraordinary place that may be the preview of things to come: the valuable reuse of things that we are accustomed to throwing away. What we arbitrarily assign as garbage is likely still of good use and value. Nothing is lacking but the creative imagination to turn it into something new.

My good friend Sister Rosemary Nyirumbe, a 2007 "CNN Superhero," has worked at a variety of orphanages and schools in East Africa. She is the headmistress at St. Monica's Girls' Tailoring School in Gulu, Uganda, while fundraising to build a similar school in one of the poorest villages in her country in a remote area called Atiak. She always seems to possess a burst of creative energy just waiting to be released. She had this house built.

The water bottle house had humble beginnings. Sister Rosemary took some foreign visitors on a short safari at Murchison Falls Game Park. Under the hot Ugandan sun, almost everyone was drinking bottled water. When they disembarked from their boat, people threw their empty bottles into the nearest trash receptacle. Rosemary's mind immediately went to work wondering about what good purpose those discarded bottles might still have. She politely asked a member of the staff where these bottles were going. He took her to a large garbage heap where plastic bottles were being melted by fire. Rosemary noted that all the trees around this burn site were dying, no doubt from the toxic fumes that burning plastic emits.

That evening Sister Rosemary noticed that everyone around her was consuming beverages from plastic bottles. By now she had a heightened awareness of the ubiquity of these throwaway bottles that she sensed still had value. By the time she returned home the next day her vehicle was loaded with more than two thousand empty water bottles. They were all destined for a new purpose, although she did not know what that purpose would be.

Sister Rosemary has been blessed to have volunteers come and work on projects alongside her from the United States and

Europe. She asked Elizabeth Moreno, a member of the Mennonite Volunteer Corp from Oregon, to research creative ways discarded plastics are being used today. After searching on Google for an afternoon, she was able to show her an assortment of findings: melted plastic jewelry, bottle furniture, seedling planters, and outdoor latrines, to name a few. Elizabeth even found that in some parts of the developing world people have been building houses using discarded plastics bottles.

Plastic bottle construction is the brainchild of Andreas Froese, a German architect and environmental entrepreneur. In 2001 Froese founded Eco-Technology, a Honduras-based environmental construction group. They pioneered a method to utilize plastic bottles as "brick" in the construction of water tanks, latrines, and houses. In ten years' time, Eco-Tech has partnered with government groups and NGOs in the construction of over fifty bottle projects across Latin America, India, and more recently, Africa.

One of the first plastic bottle construction projects in Africa began in a Ugandan village, Kayunga, located just north of the capital city, Kampala. In 2009 a community survey in the village revealed that many farmers had low crop yields due to poor soil fertility. One factor contributing to the poor fertility was the presence of waste plastics in the form of bottles and bags in the soil. The villagers took a creative approach to the problem. Kayunga had long been in need of a new latrine block for the local primary school. Some of the local leaders had recently learned of the efforts of Eco-Tech to put discarded plastics to use in new construction. The children of the school all helped gather the discarded bottles that would help form the walls of their new latrines. Constructed in April 2010, this latrine block was the first of its kind on the African continent.

Sister Rosemary invited the leaders of this project in Kayunga to come to Gulu for a week and train her and her friends on bottle construction technology. They spent hours sharing practical information along with joint reflection on the environmental benefits to their respective communities. Rosemary knows that not only are water bottles discarded in our communities; there are also "disposable people." They are looked down upon by many as weak and ineffectual persons, routinely underappreciated or ignored. Sister Rosemary sees something else in them: resilience and a yearning to contribute to building a more humane world. She deliberately chose to entrust her dream project to build this home to them. There is dignity and self-esteem present in the work opportunities that Rosemary offered. There is also a chance to earn desperately needed resources that make family life and its upkeep possible, especially the school fees. Who would not be proud of their involvement in a project building a beautiful home out of the most unlikely materials?

The first invited to share in the project was a recently widowed mother of eight. She was struggling to raise her four sets of twins without a steady source of income since her husband succumbed to the ravages of AIDS, the scourge that has stalked this continent for three decades. She herself is embracing life with the realization that she is HIV-positive. This mother in her mid-thirties was filled with delight with Sister Rosemary's request that she help fill the bottles with tightly packed soil. In return, she would be earning one hundred schillings per bottle. She daily fills bottles at home, often with the help of her children. She is now partially blind and weakens easily, often exhausted from her constant worrying about her children's future. She feels she is still able to provide concretely for her children's needs by the work Sister Rosemary gives her. Sister Rosemary was afraid this task might be too taxing for her. Rosemary assured her that she could find another income-generating project for her if this work was too physically demanding. She declined the offer, saying, "My work does not weaken me; it breathes new life into me and my family."

The gatekeeper at St. Monica's Girls' Tailoring School is an industrious young man whom Rosemary had long thought was underutilized. He and his young wife had just given birth to their firstborn, a son. He became one of the most enthusiastic collaborators in Rosemary's dream house. The first day he filled more than 240 bottles, all while fulfilling his other assigned tasks without flaw. He was thrilled to have the opportunity to do some valuable task that would help provide the needed food and shelter for his growing family. He has already begun saving bottles now to build a small home for his own family. Recently he wrote to me, "When you return to Africa next time you will find my family living in our new water bottle house. We have already collected over 3,500 bottles to use in its construction."

After Mass one Sunday morning Sister Rosemary announced to her young students, all girls in their late teens and early twenties, that she needed helpers in building the water bottle house and that in return they would receive free school supplies. She would provide them with pens, paper, and so on, in exchange for their contribution. Over thirty girls arrived together and jointly shared in the work of building this extraordinary home. All the while they were singing, telling stories, simply enjoying each other's company.

The youngest collaborator in Sister Rosemary's dream is a six-year-old boy named Innocent. He was born without arms and abandoned at birth by his parents, who saw in his physical limitations a bad omen. His uncle took him into his custody but often locked him in the house the whole day because the family was embarrassed by his looks. People constantly stared at him. They were also fearful that he might be abducted and taken away to be used in traveling sideshows. The Sisters of the Sacred Heart at St. Monica's placed him in their kindergarten and welcomed him to live among them.

On his first day working for Sister Rosemary, he filled thirty-seven water bottles, tightly packed, all with his feet.

Several communities of religious women in the United States have been ardent proponents of abolishing the practice of consuming bottled water altogether. They argue that recycling only marginally reduces the amount of resources needed to package water. There is a growing sense that the crux of the problem is excessive production and consumption of plastics, especially considering the fact that it takes a plastic water bottle hundreds of years before it decomposes. But even if it is unlikely that the production of bottled water will decrease any time soon, the story of the water bottle house still raises three important observations. First, it teaches us that appearances can be deceiving: what something is cannot be defined solely by how we regard it. If that were true, then water bottles would simply be waste (to be melted or perhaps recycled) and not precious resources. The people who constructed this house would simply be a mother with HIV, a gatekeeper, and a boy without arms. This project shows how much untapped potential there is in disposable bottles and in supposedly disposable people. We should not deceive ourselves into believing that we can so simply and conveniently define the things and, especially, the people around us.

The second lesson the water bottle house teaches us is that we must reconsider our ideas about technology if we are to develop sustainable solutions for the poorest of people. Technology, for many, means the gadgets that we buy either to make our routine tasks more convenient or to make our free time more enjoyable. Yet this project challenges those assumptions and shows us that technology simply implies human ingenuity rather than advances in electronics. Even the items we customarily throw away can be transformed through the power of human creativity. Poor countries may not have access to fancy gadgets, but they have an unending supply of ingenuity to bring about local and site-specific solutions to serious problems.

The third and final lesson from this project is that tremendous things can happen when human creativity is combined with the tenacity of people like Sister Rosemary and her unlikely team of construction workers. The ability to see the world differently is merely the beginning; the will to see the project through to the end is the difficult part. When a six-year-old boy with no arms has the determination to fill dozens of these bottles with sand, one wonders what else he could accomplish if given the opportunity. It is remarkable how proficient some of us are in finding the silver lining of a dire situation. The rest of us need only to cultivate an appreciation for possibility, instead of succumbing to the temptation that the way we think habitually accurately reflects the way things are and the way they must be.

Sister Rosemary, as a woman religious, has taken a vow of lifelong poverty. She and her community have very limited access to funds for such building projects. She must rely on the altruism and generosity of people who share her vision and commitment.

A group of US athletes, lawyers, business leaders, doctors, and professionals from various fields have formed a group known as Pros for Africa. Reggie Whitten, an Oklahoma City attorney who lost his son Brandon to drug addiction in 2001 and has since made it his life's work to help others avoid unnecessary tragedies in their lives, is one of its founders. Pros for Africa were excited to enter into a partnership with Sister Rosemary and secure the monetary means needed to see this project through to completion. Minnesota Vikings NFL running back Adrian Peterson is an active member of this group and has visited Sister Rosemary at the water bottle house in Gulu. Adrian spent his twenty-fifth birthday in Uganda with Sister Rosemary, playing with the children and enjoying teaching them a little American-style football.

Reggie Whitten's son Brandon was the child any father or mother dreams of rearing. He had a heart open to others, a trait that made him popular at Westmoore High in Oklahoma where he was homecoming king in 1995. He was a leader, a football player, a handsome young man with ambition. He wanted to be just like his dad, whom he had always admired since early child-hood. His father was a brilliant lawyer, generous in spirit, possess-ing a winning way about him. Brandon dreamed of following in his dad's footsteps and hopefully one day working side-by-side with him in the law firm. But Brandon also kept a secret from his father. For years he was accustomed to taking Valium with alcohol chasers, a dangerous habit he was introduced to while playing college football at Southwestern Oklahoma State. Only after Brandon and his girlfriend were in a major car crash did the secret emerge. Brandon's girlfriend never left the hospital. While being treated for the injuries sustained in the crash, she acquired a staph infection and died. She asked that Brandon be brought from his hospital room to hers so that she could see Brandon one last time. She just wanted to be close to him, to somehow embrace the future that they had hoped to share together.

Her death was hard for everyone to bear. Brandon felt destroyed. He was never the same after that. "It just killed him," his father relates. Afterward, Reggie sent Brandon to one of the best rehab centers available for a thirty-day recovery program. The next three years were marked by numerous relapses and emotional pain. On Valentine's Day, 2002, at twenty-five years old, Brandon was in an alcohol-related motorcycle crash that took his life and shattered the world of his family and friends. After his son's death, Reggie's life went on a fast downward spiral. He wasn't eating or sleeping. He lost weight, and his health deteriorated. He felt overwhelmed by the emotional pain of so great a loss. He stopped believing that the future bore any promise. It appeared to his friends that he was slowly dying in front of them. They decided that he needed an intervention. He needed to connect to another part of the world, to something meaningful and altogether new. About six months after Brandon's death, Reggie's friends took him to Africa. He had never been there before nor had he ever felt the yearning to go. Little could he know that the people and experiences he would encounter in Africa would soon become his lifeline.

This life-altering adventure brought him eventually to Sister Rosemary at St. Monica's in Gulu, Uganda. "Connecting to Sister Rosemary and her girls is like taking medicine for me," Reggie relates. He was suddenly caught up in the story of Sister Rosemary's outreach to formerly abducted child soldiers and young girls whom the rebels had been using as sex slaves. At St. Monica's, these girls have a chance to reclaim their lives after being kidnapped and exploited by Joseph Kony's forces. Many of those who survived the conflict returned with babies as a result of their enslavement. Reggie would connect in a personal way with the lives of Ugandans crushed by war and abuse who now were being healed and empowered to reclaim their lives. Reggie would come to be profoundly touched by these vulnerable women, sensing in them incredible frailty, on the one hand, and extraordinary depths of resilience, on the other.

With his new adventures, his personal life slowly began to take on new meanings. His new driving ambition was to try to save young people from whatever may harm them, which gives his life a newfound momentum. Reggie has inspired scores of other professionals (including practicing physicians, nurses,

attorneys, engineers, accountants, designers, carpenters, entre-
preneurs, educators, and pro athletes) to join him in sharing
their skills, their knowledge, and their friendship with some of
humanity's extremely vulnerable youth. The group Pros for Africa recently began a new creative project that draws together the
efforts of young people across the world. With Sister Rosemary's
inspiration guiding them, Sisters United was born. This business venture is designed to promote a fun and trendy global
brand of fashion. This inspired effort is all about connecting
the aspirations of women and girls in a war-torn region of
Africa to young people in relatively affluent neighborhoods
eight thousand miles away who share the same emotions, hopes,
and dreams about the future.

It is surprising both in its simplicity and the resulting beauty
it fashions: Using pop-top tabs and a little yarn from the United States, combined with the fashion sense, creativity, and hard
work of Sister Rosemary's girls in Africa, a stunning work of art
is created. Colorful handbags that are stylish, unique works of
art are made every day by young women yearning for a better
future. This remarkable project is giving hope and a chance to
have meaningful lives with dignity to young Ugandan women
who once knew only the torments of war. These youths who
live with few options are discovering that their counterparts in
the United States really do care about what comes for them
and their future after the war. Hand-crocheted together at St.
Monica's Girls' Tailoring School under the careful guidance of
Sister Rosemary and the other sisters, the end result is artwork
any woman would be proud to own. It is incredible what a
simple, successful, income-generating project can do to stir up
possibilities for more promising days ahead. Girls who were once
forced to live as sex slaves or child soldiers in Uganda are now
experiencing their innate dignity and are esteemed by others as
skilled and valued professionals.

We live in a world where billions of aluminum pop-top tab
cans are discarded each year. Sister Rosemary sees potential treasure where others see only trash. She saw empty plastic water
bottles and envisioned a house built out of them; similarly, she

and her friends saw discarded pop cans everywhere and, with a single stroke of genius, wondered if they could be made into high-quality fashion accessories that would give meaningful work to scores of young women in her hometown. Today young people from across the United States are trying to collect 6 million little pop-tabs this year alone to further this project. Yarn and pop-tabs: two simple items that bear the power to offer hope and unity to the human family.

In countless initiatives since the dawn of our new millennium, persons possessing a sense of our common humanity have taken this noble sentiment and transformed it into bridges of solidarity all across the globe, working all the while to address income disparities. The World Economic Forum convenes an impressive array of global leaders, titans of industry, senior government operatives, and leading academics of the day in the trendy Alpine resort city of Davos, Switzerland. It precedes its annual gathering by publishing a "Global Risks Report" listing the most prevalent and menacing dangers to the global community.[20] At the very top of the list in 2013 was the glaring, severe income disparity evident in so many regions of the world. There was a clear consensus that this widening chasm—the gulf between those who possess a measure of economic security offering them freedom from daily want and those locked in spheres of human deprivation reducing them to a constant struggle for survival—is directly harming the global community and placing us all at risk.

For decades, the moral vision and social teaching of the Catholic Church have vigorously offered this same core insight. The Pontifical Council for Justice and Peace captured this foundational insight in a key passage in the Compendium of the Social Doctrine of the Church:

> *If economic activity is to have a moral character, it must be directed to all men and to all peoples.* Everyone has the right to participate in economic life and the duty to contribute, each according to his own capacity, to the progress of his own country and to that of the entire human family. If, to some degree, everyone is responsible for everyone else,

then each person also has the duty to commit himself to
the economic development of all. This is a duty in solidarity and in justice, but it is also the best way to bring
economic progress to all of humanity.[21]

Just a few centuries ago, economic disparity was very different
than it is today. Prior to the Industrial Revolution, basic living
standards changed little for a millennium, and nearly everyone
was poor, with the rare exception of a few very large landowners
and aristocrats. This revolution in manufacturing, accompanied
by a mass movement of people from the farmlands to the cities, was a decisive turning point in our human story. It spurred
unprecedented growth both in our global population and in the
incomes of tens of millions of families in the more industrialized
Northern Hemisphere. Estimates hold that the world's population did not cross the threshold of the 1 billion mark until the
first decade of the nineteenth century. Since that time it has
swollen sevenfold.

In 2005 the World Bank defined extreme poverty as living on
less than $1.25 per day. The eradication of extreme poverty and
hunger was the first Millennium Development Goal set at the
United Nations by its member states at the dawn of the twenty-
first century. One in seven of us, or close to 1 billion persons, are
left trapped in extreme poverty today. Fortunately, much of the
rest of humanity possesses a level of economic security offering
them far greater freedom from the constant search for the necessities of life.

I pray nightly to God in gratitude for the freedom that my
family and I know of not ever having to search for food or
water, not wanting for a toilet, not caught in a constant worry
that our loved ones will be denied medical care when struggles
strike us. One billion of us face such dire realities every day, and
many of the rest of us are left wondering how best to respond to
the pressing needs of those who have yet to share in humanity's
great progress.

Once, in the midst of a wintry snowstorm in Cleveland, I
entered a major downtown commercial property at midday. It

housed numerous financial institutions and several renowned law firms. I entered for a single and simple reason. I had no money. I had to go to my bank and cash a check. That particular day I was not feeling well and asked a security guard where I'd find a public restroom. He curtly told me there were none anywhere. I entered my bank from the lobby, conducted my business transaction, and returned to the lobby where this same security officer approached me. He apologized saying he didn't understand that I was a customer. It was my day off from work and I was dressed down, appearing to him perhaps like I might very likely live on the city's streets. A bathroom door was opened for me immediately, with profuse apologies. I actually took little offense at this incident at the time. In retrospect, I may even have felt like I was the guilty one. Why didn't I have the sense to dress more appropriately when I choose to enter public places?

I remembered this incident several years later in full detail in a moment of personal vulnerability. It hit home to me in dramatic fashion only while I was experiencing the urgent and frequent need to use a toilet because of a health crisis. I was entering, if only briefly, the lives of precarious and powerless persons in urban India. I was in Mumbai and in Kolkata, two of the most populated cities in the Indian subcontinent, where secure sanitation is not available for nearly half a billion persons. We arrived in Mumbai on the wettest day in over two years. It seemed like the rain would never end. It was the beginning of the monsoons.

I was venturing into a world that was completely unknown to me, especially the dangers I would find afflicting me from the contagion found in the standing water in the slums. Within days I was ill and could not be very far from a toilet for the next two months. I was outside my homeland throughout those weeks, both in India, where I was struck ill, then on to East Africa. It was in Africa that I first saw a doctor in the hopes of being cured of this ailment. The clinic I visited was overwhelmed. So many people needed medical attention that many slept outside the whole night in the hopes of raising their chances of seeing a health-care professional in the morning.

Suddenly, I was now the person on the disadvantaged side of the gulf that separates the human family.

I needed a toilet.

I needed a doctor.

I needed the attention of those able to help me to be restored to health. Without being restored to health, I could no longer live a productive, meaningful life. In my vulnerability I had a brief glimpse of what our sisters and brothers in extreme poverty brutally endure each day.

Those trapped in extreme poverty can be found in all corners of the world. While Asia leads in numbers, Africa has the largest proportion—nearly half its population. Both populations often face the same systemic challenges, most especially the desperately inadequate health-care and educational systems that do not provide the health and education required for human flourishing. I have seen schools in Africa so crowded that some of the children remain outdoors all day, never even entering the building because there is no room for them. They remain standing at a window to the classroom, straining to hear the teacher's voice. Millions of people locked in extreme poverty also live in regions of our world that lack a favorable climate for growing food, few energy sources, and no access to good harbors for transporting goods. Such challenges keep them from gaining even a foothold in sustainable development.

Such entrenched poverty and the resulting challenges it creates cut across every geographical line. The United States, the world's leading economic superpower, is not exempt. US cities are likewise being ripped apart by the gnawing disparity between the top 1 percent succeeding in today's economy and the millions of families left out and trapped at the bottom. In South Bend, Indiana, home to one of the United States' educational jewels, the University of Notre Dame, 24 percent of the city's population lives below the poverty line.[22] The economic and financial crisis that engulfed the world beginning in 2008, the worst of its kind in the living memory of most Americans, occasioned for many a reexamination of our common life. This rapidly unfolding crisis changed the lives of millions of people, unveiling the tenuous ties that bind. These ties were frayed by serious economic pressures, and the powerfully divisive forces at play in the economic and political spheres continue to the present day.

Because such economic hardship and suffering are outside the experience of many Americans, many were unsure if they were equipped to deal with the onslaught. For the first time, many people in the United States experienced a profound sense of vulnerability. Those who rarely had to make sacrifices in the past were left wondering how they were going to meet their mortgage obligations, pay escalating medical costs, and keep food on the table for their children and grandchildren. The significant structural problems facing the global economy cannot be easily resolved. They call for a renewal of civic life. How ought that crisis of moral meaning and solidarity in our world be resolved and the good society advanced? What new moral and social possibilities offer themselves in the present moment as uniquely and decisively capable of transforming our world into a more compassionate and just community?

A fundamental challenge is the need for a genuine and ongoing renewal of civic virtue, with its accompanying sense of the rights and responsibilities of citizenship. Our religious leaders are uniquely poised to offer the moral vision and voice to lift us all to see our stake in each other's well-being. Robert Reich, a former US secretary of labor and one of our world's most innovative political economists, underscores in his writings the pressing need to connect individuals with what is at stake, namely, the common good of all. He writes, "Individuals comprising a society will sacrifice their personal well-being to the greater good only if they feel connected to that society in such a way that 'the greater good' has substantive meaning for them."[23]

The most genuine hope for a more just and humane society involves recognizing the need to recast the basis of social and economic life. That recasting is framed by a movement away from "the disintegrating tendencies of commercial society"[24] toward

a reinvigorated commitment to the vital moral understandings
that bind a society together. One of the most crucial moral perspectives on justice that is capable of enhancing social solidarity
is the notion of justice as participation. The US bishops, in their
economic pastoral letter of 1986, linked the virtue of justice with
the capacity to participate: "Justice demands that social institutions be ordered in a way that guarantees all persons the ability
to participate actively in the economic, political, and cultural
life of society. . . . Such participation is an essential expression of
the social nature of human beings and of their communitarian
vocation."[25]

Jesuit theologian Drew Christiansen suggests that over the
past several decades of societal evolution, "The American tradition has come to identify a number of limitations inherent
in the pursuit of interest as a principle of social organization
and of politics."[26] Among these limitations is the consistent
devaluing within society of many of the fundamental needs that
US citizens share that are not joined directly to an autonomous
self-interest. One such need is to expand our capacity to define
the common good. Christiansen writes, "True politics cannot
be pursued by consulting one's own interest, like a hungry man
filling his stomach or an accountant looking for a higher quar-
terly return. Rather, politics, as the highest form of social living,
entails 'critical self-reflection' so that we can identify 'what all
can want.'"[27]

The kind of critical self-reflection that is capable of iden-
tifying "what all can want" is unlikely to develop without an
atmosphere of civic amity. This echoes the fundamental insights
of Aristotle, who, in his *Nicomachean Ethics*,[28] pleads for such civic
amity within the Greek polis. Berkeley sociologist James Stockinger eloquently captures what it means to be dependent upon
one another. He does so through a reflection on the movements
of hands:

> For each of us lives in and through an immense move-
> ment of the hands of other people. The hands of other
> people lift us from the womb. The hands of other people

grow the food we eat, weave the clothes we wear and build the shelters we inhabit. The hands of other people give pleasure to our bodies in moments of passion and aid and comfort in times of affliction and distress. It is in and through the hands of other people that the commonwealth of nature is appropriated and accommodated to the needs and pleasures of our separate, individual lives, and, at the end, is it the hands of other people that lower us into the earth.[29]

Orestes A. Brownson was a highly influential nineteenth-century American scholar, versed in the fields of theology, economics, education, and politics, who embraced Catholicism in 1844. He often grappled with the idea of civic duty. Embracing his own sense of duty to the vulnerable, Brownson pleaded for a US government that would curtail its deferential treatment of the rich and the powerful and focus instead on the implementation of social and economic relationships capable of enhancing social solidarity and advancing the common good. Of paramount concern for Brownson was the need for civic duty to offer new possibilities and alternative social choices capable of countering the social fragmentation of his day. In 1843 Orestes Brownson was invited to speak at the graduation exercises for Dartmouth College. His address on that occasion illuminates his understanding of what civic duty entails. He exhorted his audience to this virtue in these words: "Ask not what your age wants, but what it needs; not what it will reward, but what without which it cannot be saved; and that, go and do; do it well; do it thoroughly; and find your reward in the consciousness of having done your duty."[30]

    The call to civic duty paramount in his vision of social and economic justice well over a century ago appears again in reflections offered by our US Catholic bishops. In the document "Economic Justice for All," the US bishops claim that the rediscovery of this civic friendship is a key element in increasing participation within the economic and social realms of those who are marginalized. The bishops urge owners and managers, those who wield considerable power in the shaping of the economic institutions on which our common life depends, to embrace civic duty by seeing their positions of responsibility as a vocation, rather than merely a job or occupation. The bishops state, "Persons in management face many hard choices each day, choices on which the well-being of many others depends. Commitment to the public good and not simply the private good of their firms is at the heart of what it means to call their work a vocation and not simply a career or a job."[31] Brownson identified an innate human desire to positively influence the broader community by being attentive to the deeper aspirations of the human person: "As soon as men find themselves well off in a worldly point of view, they discover that they have wants which the world does not and cannot satisfy. The training demanded to ensure success in commerce, industrial enterprises, or politics, strengthens faculties which crave something superior to commerce, to mere industry, or to politics."[32]

How do we urge owners and managers of corporations to view the power and the wealth that their positions create as a gift held in trust? The wealth that has been generated has come forward not solely through their personal initiatives and achievements but must also be seen as having been created through the workings of community: "Resources created by human industry are also held in trust. Owners and managers have not created this capital on their own. They have benefited from the work of many others and from the local communities that support their endeavors."[33] The Christian vision of our economic life stresses that those possessing greater wealth, those gifted with professional and technical skills needed to enhance the lives of others, and those charged with the tasks and responsibilities of government all have a greater duty to make a positive contribution to the lives of others.

Notes

[1] From the foreword to *The Nazi Doctors and the Nuremberg Code: Human Rights in Human Experimentation*, ed. George Annas and Michael Grodin (New York: Oxford University Press, 1992).

[2] Father Placido Fonseca, *Tracks* (n.p., 2007), 67.

[3] Stephen Marche, "Is Facebook Making Us Lonely?" *The Atlantic,* April 2, 2012.

[4] "Semester Abroad Spent Drinking with Other American Students," *The Onion,* issue 38–05, February 13, 2012.

[5] John Kavanaugh, "Autonomous Individualism," *America,* January 15, 2007.

[6] Ibid.

[7] Ibid.

[8] Many of his books and essays are worth reading, but it might be helpful to start with the following: Amartya Sen, *Development as Freedom* (New York: Random House, 1999)

[9] Katherine Boo, *Behind the Beautiful Forevers* (New York: Random House, 2012), epigraph to part 1.

[10] See *The Preferential Option for the Poor,* ed. Richard John Neuhaus (New York: Eerdmans, 1988).

[11] *Tracks,* 29.

[12] See John Rawls, *A Theory of Justice* (Cambridge, MA: Harvard University Press, 1971).

[13] See Robert Nozick, *Anarchy, State, and Utopia* (New York: Basic Books, 1974).

[14] A PDF of the essay is available at http://people.brandeis.edu/~teuber/Clifford_ethics.pdf.

[15] See *Spiritual Exercises of Saint Ignatius,* trans. Anthony Mottola (New York: Image Books, 1989), exercise #23.

[16] Robert Skidelsky and Edward Skidelsky, "In Praise of Leisure," *Chronicle of Higher Education,* June 18, 2012.

[17] Ibid.

[18] Jeff Tietz, "The Fallen," *Rolling Stone,* July 2012, 90–99, 114.

[19] See "The Holocaust: Crimes, Hereoes, and Villains," http://www.auschwitz.dk/.

[20] "Global Risks 2013," 8th ed., http://www.weforum.org/reports/global-risks-2013-eighth-edition.

[21] Pontifical Council for Justice and Peace, *Compendium of the Social Doctrine of the Church,* para. 333 (emphasis in original).

[22] "QuickFacts from the U.S. Census Bureau," http://quickfacts.census.gov/qfd/states/18/187000.html.

[23] Robert B. Reich, *The Work of Nations: Preparing Ourselves for Twenty-First-Century Capitalism* (New York: Vintage Books, 1992), 317.

[24] William Sullivan, *Reconstructing Public Philosophy* (Berkeley: University of California Press, 1986), 14.

[25] National Conference of Catholic Bishops, "Economic Justice for All: Catholic Social Teaching and the U.S. Economy," *Origins* 16 (November 1986), 420, para. 78 [hereafter referred to as *EJA*].

[26] Drew Christiansen, "The Common Good and the Politics of Self-Interest," in *Beyond Individualism: Toward a Retrieval of Moral Discourse in America*, ed. Donald Gelpi (Notre Dame, IN: University of Notre Dame Press, 1989), 74.

[27] Ibid.

[28] Aristotle, *The Nicomachean Ethics*, William David Ross, ed. (Oxford: Oxford University Press, 1980), 192–219.

[29] James Stockinger, as quoted by Robert Bellah et al. in *The Good Society* (New York: Alfred A. Knopf, 1991), 104. These words were extracted from Stockinger's unpublished PhD dissertation, "Locke and Rousseau: Human Nature, Human Citizenship, and Human Work," Department of Sociology, University of California, Berkeley.

[30] Orestes A. Brownson, as quoted by James Malone in "Relating Church Moral Teaching to Politics," *Origins* 15 (1986): 607.

[31] *EJA*, 423–24, para. 111.

[32] Orestes A. Brownson, as found in *Orestes A. Brownson: Selected Writings*, ed. Patrick W. Carey (Mahwah, NJ: Paulist, 1991), 183.

[33] *EJA*, 424, para. 113.

Chapter 6

The Problem of Evil and the Limits of Human Control

The fact of suffering undoubtedly constitutes the single greatest challenge to the Christian faith, and has been in every generation. Its distribution and degree appear to be entirely random and therefore unfair. Sensitive spirits ask if it can possibly be reconciled with God's justice and love.

—*John Stott*[1]

Jim

I was in college when I first read Fyodor Dostoevsky's *The Brothers Karamazov*, and it had a profound impact on me. Dostoevsky speaks through the two most important characters, Ivan and Alyosha. The brothers engage in a series of philosophical and theological discussions. Ivan is a twenty-four-year-old avowed atheist who cannot fathom why an all-powerful and all-good God would allow the innocent to suffer. Alyosha is a twenty-year-old novice monk who, though no less thoughtful or sensitive, is comfortable turning to faith when his own understanding does not suffice. Ivan accuses Christians of being complicit with innocent suffering, alleging that they invent elaborate rationalizations that "falsify the facts."[2] By believing in an all-powerful, all-good God, Christians fall back on pithy phrases like "It's all in God's plan." Humans, not being omniscient, cannot comprehend this plan. Yet our lack of understanding does not make the plan, the eternal harmony of God's will, any less real. Ivan, on the contrary, insists that innocent suffering cannot be part of a plan of a God that is supposed to be both all-powerful and all-good. Innocent suffering is simply absurd, and we should acknowledge its absurdity instead of attempting to explain it away.

According to Ivan, another failed explanation for evil in the world is the concept of free will. This idea has been used to show the compatibility of a perfect God and a horribly imperfect world. The presence of evil is not God's fault, but ours, for we are the ones who abuse the gift of free will by harming others.[3] Yet Ivan points out that this supposed gift has more often been a curse, and he wonders whether the benefits of being free have outweighed the terrible costs, especially when God's free people are also fallen and flawed by nature. Wouldn't an all-knowing God recognize that the vast majority of people would be too weak to be free? To Ivan, this all seems like a cosmic joke.

Alyosha listens carefully to his brother's views, occasionally interjecting a remark. At the end of one of Ivan's speeches, Alyosha kisses his brother without comment. It becomes clear to the reader that, in spite of everything Ivan has said, Alyosha's faith is steadfast. Some might say that Ivan deserves a thoughtful response to the dilemma he poses. After all, he is accusing Christians like his own brother of being complicit with the suffering of innocent people, and this suffering is built into the very nature of the world God has created; it cannot be adequately combated by doing charity work on the weekends. On the other hand, Alyosha's faith might be regarded as a deep belief that human understanding cannot grasp God's will. If this is so, then arguing with Ivan would be futile. There is nothing to say and nothing that really could be said.

Regardless of whether Ivan is owed an explanation, or whether a genuine one is even possible, his views reinforce what Hannah Arendt has called "the banality of evil."[4] To call something "banal" is to say that it is common and conventional. Arendt coined the phrase in her book *Eichmann in Jerusalem*, which examined the horrific crimes committed not by fanatics but by ordinary people who simply followed orders. What if it were true that most of what counts as evil in the world often goes unnoticed? What if most of these evil acts were committed by ordinary people? If this were so, then evil would be radical in addition to being banal. In other words, it would form a basic part of the human condition and would be deeply resistant to calls for solidarity.

Ivan offers numerous and graphic examples of ordinary innocent suffering, but one need not read fiction to find such cases. Sometimes I play racquetball with a US Marine charged with training Mexico's special-operations troops to fight drug cartels. Despite the fact that Mexico is our immediate neighbor to the south, most people in the United States are blissfully unaware of the violence perpetrated by these groups, even as they buy the drugs that fund the war. After our match I asked him how his work was going. The soldier mentioned that he had recently seen a tape depicting the torture and killing of a sixteen-year-old Mexican soldier. When he tried to reflect on the meaning of the video, he was at a loss for words. He was unable to make sense of how one human being could do that to another, especially a near-child. And what he found especially disturbing was that the torturers were probably just ordinary human beings whose lives took a bizarre turn toward violence. They were likely interested exclusively in cash, but how could money sufficiently motivate one human being to do that to another?

If evil is ordinary, then are we simply (and sadly) morally blind? Is there a cure for moral blindness that does not require a miracle? As much as we might praise Alyosha for his deep and abiding faith, it is hard not to sympathize with Ivan, the man who either wants a genuine explanation for the rampant evil in the world or an end to convenient rationalizations for evil actions.

Whatever solidarity means, and however evil is to be combated, we must regard it as a daily challenge, as a necessary part of our own spiritual and intellectual self-formation. We must not be self-indulgent occasional Christians, nor must we be defeated atheists who dismiss the human condition as simply absurd. *Whether Ivan is right or not is beside the point.* The gift of freedom can be used appropriately as well as it can be abused. Calling something "absurd" does not diminish its effects, and only those who cultivate an awareness of the banality of evil will notice it enough to fight it. In his encyclical "On Social Concerns," Pope John Paul II eloquently expresses this point. He defines solidarity "not [as] a feeling of vague compassion or shallow distress at the misfortunes of so many people, both near and far. On the contrary, it is *a firm and persevering determination* to commit oneself to the *common good*; that is to say to the good of all and of each individual, because we are *all* really responsible *for all*."[5] While we must remember that it is often difficult to determine the best way of helping someone, the idea of a "firm and persevering determination" captures something important about this idea. Pope John Paul II insists that true solidarity depends upon a change in *"spiritual attitudes* which define each individual's relationship with self, with neighbor, with even the remotest human communities, and with nature itself."[6] He even refers to this as a kind of conversion experience, a fundamental shift in consciousness, which requires the ongoing cultivation of one's judgment and the rejection of superficial solutions.

Father Placie, the director of the Indian organization that places street children in foster homes, hints at several ways in which we should cultivate our judgment. First, he rejects the religious stereotype that Ivan targeted when he accused believers of being complicit with suffering, writing, "It's easy to say, 'Those whom the Gods love, die young,' but when we know that there are children who have died because nobody loved them, nobody cared enough to make a difference . . . it's time to stop with the proverbs and accept reality."[7] Then he exhorts his readers, "Let us make our street children visible again."[8] So the first way of cultivating one's judgment is simply to notice what normally escapes our attention.

The second way is to approach problems thoughtfully, with the full realization of their complexity. Decades of dealing with runaway children has attuned him to the nuances of each case, for no two cases are alike. He writes, "Children determined to eke out a living here, or set on being away from their families will use their imaginations to tell stories calculated to tug at your heartstrings."⁹ Children with especially vivid imaginations can construct a completely fictional past. Unless Father Placie can see through the illusion, he will place someone's beloved but runaway child in a different home. He faces an equally tough moral challenge when he attempts to reunite a child with his or her family. Is this family environment suitable for the child? Is the father or mother violent, or is the parents' discipline within the acceptable realm of parenting practices?

True solidarity is hopeful, determined, and realistic about the fundamental limitations in human nature and about the ability to effect change. Although it soberly recognizes these limitations, it does not use them as excuses. Consider, for example, the possibility of a major pharmaceutical company discovering a cure for AIDS. Suppose the cure was discovered as a result of tests conducted in Africa. Although the people might have been compensated in a way (e.g., some food for their families), questions remain about how to ensure access to the drug for those who need it. For the most part, they have no chance of affording the drug, even at a steep discount. Should a precondition of conducting research in Africa be the distribution of a cure to the people of Africa?

A false form of solidarity would simply affirm the common good and insist that the answer is yes. But the relevant question is not whether it would be good for Africans to have access. That question is too simple and the answer too easy. The real question is twofold: (1) what tradeoffs would have to be made if the pharmaceutical companies were compelled to give away the results of their research, and (2) is it even feasible to distribute such valuable drugs when some African governments are corrupt? The vast majority of research utterly fails to produce successful drugs. This means that the drug companies' profit motive is not a simple sign of greed but rather an acknowledgment that, in the rare case when they find a cure, they must benefit financially. Research and development is costly, whether it is successful or not. The idea that a drug company could have intellectual property rights over a cure for AIDS might be unpalatable. But it seems clear that, without these rights, there probably would not be a cure in the first place.

The complicated ethics of research does not even address the deeper problem of distributing a cure once it exists. If it is already difficult to guarantee that relief supplies will make it to the people, consider the logistical nightmare of getting AIDS patients a cure. Is it morally wrong to bribe a corrupt government, or is it the cost of doing business? True solidarity means asking hard questions and refusing self-satisfied and superficial answers.

Perhaps for this reason ethicists like Peter Singer have received so much criticism. Singer's observation that geography is not morally relevant seems straightforward and true. It really should not matter whether a starving child lives down the street or in Indonesia. Hunger is hunger. Yet his view fails to recognize the moral complexity of the situation and some fundamental limitations in human nature that we have already discussed. And if Singer is right, then isn't our obligation to others infinite? After all, there will always be another hungry person to help, and there would never be a definite and nonarbitrary way of distinguishing one obligation from another. In a controversial article titled "Moral Saints," Susan Wolf objects to this kind of moral perfectionism.[10] She thinks it is obvious that, as flesh-and-blood human beings and not just moral consciences, we value lots of other elements of the human experience. If our moral obligation to others is infinite, these other basic values would diminish or even disappear altogether.

For example, suppose I had an immense talent and irrepressible urge to play the piano (neither of these is true, unfortunately). One can imagine Singer lecturing me about my moral obligations to others I will never meet, perhaps even inventing imaginative and logically compelling scenarios to make his point. Suppose, so moved, I skip practice to volunteer at a soup kitchen downtown. The next day I eagerly sit down to practice the piano and Singer returns. He reminds me that the people I helped to feed yesterday are hungry again. Also, they have some friends down the street who did not eat yesterday. And there are millions of total strangers thousands of miles away who didn't eat either.

Would it be wrong to give up playing the piano in order to attend to my infinite obligation to others? Even if this were the morally right course of action, Wolf thinks we would intuitively reject such an outcome. Such a single-minded pursuit of the common good might seem saintly, but someone who completely sacrifices his talents and interests in this way is more likely to be seen as pathological. The human experience is a big tent: it requires a balancing act between lots of competing goods and goals. Art that enriches oneself and makes the world more beautiful deserves a place in this tent, even if it comes at the expense of helping others from time to time.

A classic example of these sorts of trade-offs can be found in the life of the famous French artist Gauguin. He traveled extensively but eventually abandoned his family, moved to Tahiti, and found his inspiration in the form of beautiful women and beaches. Was it morally wrong to leave his family? Of course it was. Still, if you could somehow go back in time to make sure he was a good husband and father, would you? If you are not a fan of his art, then the answer is clearly yes. It is telling that this is a relevant consideration. If you think his art is wonderful, even irreplaceable, then the answer might be no. From a moral perspective, the answer is obvious, but from a perspective that seeks to weigh a number of competing and sometimes mutually exclusive goods and goals, the answer is unclear. Perhaps Gauguin would have been a great artist even if he had stayed at home and never seen Tahiti. But there is a difference between being technically proficient and being great, and much of an artist's greatness undoubtedly depends upon the circumstances that inspire or fail one to do so.

Great art often comes from pain, or at least from morally dubious sources of inspiration. Suppose you could travel back in time with a therapist and a bottle of antidepressants to visit Van Gogh or Hemingway. Granted, there is no cure for depression, only a number of strategies for coping with it. Still, suppose you could ease the pain that resulted, perhaps inevitably, in suicide. You might be morally required to do so, but a happy (medicated?) Van Gogh is not likely to paint potato farmers. A sedated

Hemingway could not write *The Sun Also Rises.* Would this be a small price to pay for doing the right thing, or would it be a bridge too far? Would you require Hemingway and Van Gogh to endure their internal suffering so that their great art might see the light of day? Wolf's insight is that moral perfectionism is neither possible nor desirable. Real life requires making complex and often painful trade-offs. We simply are not (nor should we be) moral saints; it would be better and more honest to recognize not only our limitations but also our other valuable nonmoral pursuits.

The question of what is in our control and what is not is a persistent and difficult question in Catholic ethics. In fact, any sort of Christian view that advocates a "What would Jesus do?" philosophy must always come with a caveat: even if, contrary to Wolf's claims, we should strive to be morally perfect like Christ, we are fundamentally human through and through. Although we are free, we are also fallen and flawed. This is what Dostoevsky's Ivan found so reprehensible about the human condition: we are created weak but expected to use our free will responsibly. It makes sense to say that some things are up to us and some are not. How, then, can we determine what we are responsible for and what we are not?

This question features prominently in Catholic discussions of moral dilemmas in medical ethics. Whenever I teach medical ethics, we discuss controversial issues like prenatal testing, genetic enhancement, and even cloning. One standard Catholic view on these topics is that technology tempts us to transgress the moral limits of human control. While prenatal testing is the least controversial practice of the three just mentioned, it strikes some Catholic ethicists as the attempt to discern (in utero) whether the child will be "defective." Some regard it as a precursor to genetic abortion—the deliberate killing of the fetus based on its genetic traits. Genetic enhancement is more controversial, since it seems like parents are picking and choosing traits for their children. Parents have the moral duty to love their children unconditionally, not to construct a child as if they were visiting a Build-a-Bear store. Cloning is the most controversial of the three practices, since it seems like the culmination of a disturbing trend to seize control over the very ingredients of life.

C. S. Lewis's remarkable essay "The Abolition of Man" warns us of the differences between controlling nature (the world around us) and controlling *human* nature.[11] He points out that, while the idea of progress assumes an increase in future freedom and autonomy, many actual uses of technology lead to a loss of control in the future. For instance, reproductive technologies promise the possibility of sex without pregnancy. While it looks like this dramatically increases human freedom, it actually makes the very existence of future persons dependent upon the whims of present people. Lewis's point is that technology never increases freedom generally, but only for some to the detriment of others. Other technologies, like genetic engineering, clearly make the future generation dependent upon the present like never before. We are offered the illusion of becoming self-made, but when we obliterate the idea of what is natural for the sake of progress, we no longer have any way of restricting how we can reshape our own nature. Then all moral limits fall away, too: the privileged few who have access to technologies like genetic modification have only their own preferences to inform their decisions about how to wield this awesome new power.

Lewis is part of a long line of Christian philosophers who stress the limits of human control, but it is interesting to see how this insight is used. Recall the disbelief of Dostoevsky's Ivan that an all-good, all-powerful God would allow innocent suffering. The classic response to this problem of evil is to say that God gave human beings free will. Therefore, humans, and not God, are responsible for evil. But, as Ivan points out, God made us free. So this raises some related questions: Who is ultimately responsible for suffering, and if humans are (because they are free but also fallen and flawed), then how can they also be responsible for eradicating something that is a fundamental part of the human condition?

When it comes to moral dilemmas in medicine, one standard Catholic response is that human beings are essentially limited by their own nature; they must accept rather than transgress these limitations. Yet when dealing with questions of social justice, human beings are supposed to be free and responsible for innocent suffering. As we have seen, they can even be counted as responsible through their complicit inaction. But why do we treat these issues as so radically different? In other words, why must we accept our natural limitations in one case while, in the other case, we must appreciate the fact that our freedom and responsibility are, in a sense, absolute? In one case, we are acting irresponsibly if we attempt to change our very nature, but in the other case we are expected to fight tooth and nail against our very nature. If we don't, we are guilty of condoning injustice, either through our actions or our inaction. Ivan's mistake is to say that religious people can simply say that suffering is part of God's will. In fact, they are theologically committed to accepting their own responsibility and their own freedom to change it. But is this view coherent?

Perhaps one might object that we are only responsible for mitigating suffering to the best of our ability. Once we are confident that we have done our best, we cannot be held responsible for the final outcome. For instance, we might give someone money for a meal, but we cannot determine what this person ultimately uses the money for. This would also mean accepting that inequality arising from the differences between individuals is a basic fact of the human condition. But how are we supposed to draw the fine line between our responsibility to mitigate and our duty to eradicate injustice? Might this sometimes be a recipe for rationalizing a halfhearted commitment to helping others?

Suppose someone continues to donate money to a charity rumored to commit fraud. Wouldn't we want to say that the donor was acting irresponsibly, even if the idea of giving money to the poor is morally praiseworthy? It seems dishonest to claim that once I write the check, I am not at all responsible for how the money is used. Once I learn how the money is being used, I become complicit if I continue to donate recklessly. Maybe this also means I have a duty to become informed to the extent that this is possible. If this is so, then "trying my best" turns out to be a high moral standard indeed. Sometimes it might even be identical with solving a particular moral problem. Take, for instance, the number of people who go hungry in any given city in America. We lack the collective will, not the resources, to feed these people. Anyone who makes a small contribution and then claims to have tried his best is either morally dishonest or fails to see the scope of the problem. In other words, sometimes truly trying our hardest might really mean solving a problem, such that there is no meaningful difference between mitigating and eradicating injustice.

As we have already seen in our discussion of moral perfectionism, there is always more work to be done. Consequently, there is always another obligation to consider. Perhaps we should start by ending hunger in major US cities. Would accomplishing this even be sufficient? Is it enough for someone not to starve, or do we have a moral duty to aim higher? Once we intervene in the lives of others, don't we seem to acquire new obligations as a result? If, for example, I were to volunteer as a part of Big Brothers and Big Sisters, I would take on brand-new responsibility as a mentor for a child. Although I might have had some abstract obligation to this child before meeting him, I am obligated in a very real and specific way when I promise to take him to the park. Where does our obligation to others end? If our moral obligation to others is limited in some way, how can we draw this fine line?

Why do so many Catholic ethicists seem to think that this fine line is easy to draw in medical ethics, when it is so difficult to distinguish in the case of solidarity? It is too simple to say that, in the case of the medical dilemmas, humans are using technology for morally prohibited ends, while, in the case of poverty relief, they are using their freedom for righteous ends. It is too easy to claim that using technology to change our very nature is presumptuous and morally dangerous, since the reason that new technology is so seductive is the promise it holds for healing the sick and even eradicating specific diseases. Suppose, in the not-so-distant future, you have a three-year-old child who needs a bone marrow transplant in order to live. Every potential donor is a failed match, so you consider the possibility of cloning a healthy match. You realize that creating life in order to harvest some bone marrow seems wrong. But you also intend to raise the cloned child as your own, and you are even excited about having another child. In this case, the cloned child would be a medical miracle, a hero whose very existence saved his older "brother."[12] Whether you think this is a logical argument or a mere rationalization, it seems clear that the circumstances of the specific case matter a lot.

Or think for a moment about the idea of genetic engineering. Is it really so clear that modifying genes transgresses a sacred moral limitation on what is natural? If the ultimate point of genetic modification is to determine the future appearance and behavior of the child, then surely we cannot do this with any degree of certainty. Intelligence, for instance, is likely some extremely complicated combination of genes and environment. And insofar as it is genetic, we are likely to find a number of genetic contributions, rather than a single gene, that constitute what we call intelligence. So the strong distinction between what is natural and what is unnatural might be rooted in an unsupported assumption that genes determine our behavior, such that modifying them changes me in a way that a change in my environment does not.

The idea that I can genetically determine my child's height so that he can eventually make millions playing professional basketball ignores thousands of other significant factors upon which his success depends. And to the extent that fortune plays a role, we cannot scientifically control for it. Where do the will to succeed and the competitive fire to rise above dire circumstances come from? Would Michael Jordan have been half the player he was if he was content to lose from time to time?[13] Would Kobe Bryant have enjoyed half of his success if he took a break during the off-season? If we cannot even say whether a crucial trait is genetic or the effect of environment (it is probably, in most cases, both), then distinguishing between the natural and unnatural will be difficult.

What about the millions of ways that parents attempt to modify the appearance and behavior of their children every day?

Is dyeing a child's hair as morally repugnant as determining it in the womb? Is having a child spend years wearing braces to fix his or her teeth morally equivalent to attempting to do this genetically? Since human beings are an intricate combination of nature and nurture, why condemn behaviors that only deal with half of the equation? I might be regarded as a thoughtful and responsible parent for signing my child up for basketball camp, but this is also an attempt to modify my child in a specific way.

Is the crucial moral difference that he can always decide not to play basketball, whereas he could not choose to be short if he was engineered to be tall? But going to basketball camp is more likely to make me a better player than simply being tall. So intervening on the side of nurture seems ironically more invasive than modifying genetically. And even if the decision to engineer a tall child is more permanent than two weeks at basketball camp, it is not necessarily connected to any particular behavior in a permanent fashion. Perhaps it forecloses a few possibilities (e.g., being a jockey or an Olympic gymnast), but does it do so in a morally reprehensible way? Why should we assume that changes in the environment have fewer permanent consequences than genetic modifications? Maybe we should consult a psychiatrist who makes a living by helping patients deal with the lasting (even lifelong) effects of environmental modifications!

What is the actual moral force of saying that something is unnatural? A good example is the debate over embryonic stem cell research. The question posed in this debate is whether it is morally wrong to create embryos in order to harvest stem cells for the purpose of researching cures for disease? The debate is likely moot, now that adult stem cells have shown such promise when it comes to curing disease. But we prefer adult stem cells to embryonic stem cells not because they are more natural; rather, they do not raise the same moral objections regarding the sanctity of life. The key concept in the debate over embryonic stem cells was the definition of human life (i.e., do embryos have the same moral status as persons?), not the idea of what is natural.

It seems that all medicine (at least in the West) is in some sense unnatural, but it does not follow that we would condemn the healing of the sick. If medicine is unnatural, what about the illness it tries to cure? Is a cancer cell natural or unnatural? It is easy to say that we should let nature take its course, but we also fight against the effects of nature tooth and nail until we determine it is hopeless. Establishing a consensus for when to stop treatment and move to palliative care (and a hospice setting) is far from obvious in many cases.

Maybe calling something unnatural really means that human intervention would disrupt a just and fair arrangement. In the case of genetic modification, we might think that the use of modern technology should not unfairly privilege the few who have access to it. No doubt this is an important concern, but does it mean that genetic modification leads, in principle, to a more unjust world? Perhaps we don't fully realize the sorts of commitments we have when we condemn the use of new technology to transform human nature. We worry about interfering with what is natural, but why is the genetic lottery any more just and fair than human intervention? As we have already seen, Rawls stresses just how much our lives are determined by fortune. Considering one's advantages to be blessings instead of accidents doesn't help matters either. The wildly unequal distribution of talents and desirable traits (whether by divine plan, fortune, or fate) seems sensible only from the perspective of those who do not suffer. In other words, it is easy for those who are genetically gifted to condemn the idea of genetic modification, but why letting nature take its course leads to a more just and fair outcome in general is not clear.

Michael Sandel, an American political philosopher, offers an eloquent defense of the genetic lottery against the idea of genetic enhancement.[14] He claims that using technology to transform our nature would undercut key moral elements of human relationships. For instance, in a world without this technology, those with considerable genetic gifts must develop the humility to recognize that these gifts were unearned. The conclusion they are supposed to draw is that they should use these gifts to help others, since everything could have been otherwise. The genetic lottery similarly promotes solidarity, since the seemingly random distribution of skills means that we need each other. Finally, it forces us to distinguish between what we are truly responsible for and what eludes our control. If we could genetically enhance human beings, they could presumably be held responsible for not fulfilling the purpose for which they were conceived.

The problem with Sandel's view is simple. Claiming that the genetically fortunate *must* acquire the virtues of humility, solidarity, and responsibility is no guarantee that they actually will. Recall the quote made famous by Ann Richards: "Some people are born on third base and go through life thinking they hit a triple." If this is so, then doesn't the rampant injustice in the world far outweigh the moral lessons that we (often fruitlessly) hope some fortunate people learn? If, as a matter of fact, those who are privileged do not recognize the source of their advantage, then doesn't Sandel's objection lose all of its moral force? Is the possibility of enlightening those who are fortunate (but self-deceived) a good enough reason not to tamper with the effects of the genetic lottery?

The common thread to these reflections on the natural and unnatural can be formulated in the following question: what, in the final analysis, are we in control of and responsible for, and what transcends the limits of human freedom and responsibility? This question is perhaps the most puzzling of all. Earlier we discussed several ways in which we must cultivate our judgment in order to promote true solidarity. Becoming a citizen of the world depends fundamentally on understanding what is in our control and what is not. We cannot be obligated to do something that is outside of our control, and we cannot shirk a responsibility when we could successfully solve a problem. The question, though, is whether the kind of suffering that prompts calls for solidarity is a problem to be solved or a basic feature of human nature. To the extent that this problem can be resolved, what are the limits of our responsibility to others? How will we know when our work is done?

A perfect expression of these types of concerns can be found in the Serenity Prayer: "God, grant me the serenity to accept the things I cannot change, the courage to change the things I can, and the wisdom to know the difference."[15] Simply brooding about the absurdity of injustice, as Dostoevsky's character Ivan seems to do, leads to unhappiness without changing anything. So courageous action is necessary, but, as we have seen, there are many ways in which courageous action can be hopelessly misguided and self-defeating. Wisdom is required not only for discerning the right course of action but also for determining whether action is called for in the first place.

One potential hazard of the Serenity Prayer, however, is that it offers us a way of rationalizing our own inaction. When are we making excuses for ourselves, failing to recognize a responsibility we actually have? When have we wisely determined that something is out of our control? When are we serene, and when are we merely complacent? If the Serenity Prayer helps us to make sense of solidarity as a belief and as the outcome of daily spiritual exercise, it might also mislead us into thinking that considering our beliefs is sufficient (i.e., to the detriment of our actions). A complicated example arises from this observation: Can I be in solidarity with someone else through prayer alone? Insofar as prayer is a kind of action, then perhaps I can. Yet suffering also requires a massive economic and political solution.

Perhaps this dilemma posed by the Serenity Prayer is perfectly ordinary: it is the challenge of every parent attempting to educate a child and foster a sense of self-worth and self-reliance. In his discussion of raising so-called street children at Snehasadan, Father Placie adopts an attitude that is charmingly uncertain about the efficacy of his own actions. He writes, "What baffles me at times is that the children I expect the most from have often let me down. While the boys and girls who I thought would need almost lifelong sustenance, have showed me their true grit and determination. It's life's lesson for me; never measure all children with the same yardstick."[16]

Last year I taught a freshman seminar course based on a novel called *The Other Wes Moore*.[17] This captivating book tells the story of two young men growing up in Baltimore under difficult conditions. One grows up to be a Rhodes scholar while the other serves a life sentence for murder. Despite their shared background, and even their shared name, their lives take wildly divergent paths. There are some hints as to why one young man made it while the other did not. Chief among these is the fact that one Wes was sent away to military school where he learned discipline and eventually thrived. But even this fact cannot fully explain the differences between these two seemingly similar people. What about Wes made it possible for him to excel in that environment, when there was little to no prior evidence suggesting he would?

For all of Father Placie's efforts, the outcome is surprisingly unpredictable. It is no less difficult to turn away older children and adults who return to Snehasadan after falling on hard times: "Right now, children believe Snehasadan will take care of them for life. We have to make sure that every child realizes that our homes are an opportunity to make a clean start all over again and that they have to take this opportunity and work hard at it."[18] Father Placie, like any good parent, had to learn through experience when to intervene in the lives of others and when to let go. After centuries of speculation about the proper way to raise and educate children, human development is still, at its core, mysterious and unpredictable.[19] So is solidarity in its truest sense, since its effects cannot be determined in advance. The Serenity Prayer captures this sense of uncertainty, counseling the cultivation of a humble but thoughtful response to it.

The challenge of genuinely thinking about solidarity and the challenge of living this way go hand in hand. As we have seen, it is difficult enough to gain the perspective on our own lives to start thinking like a citizen of the world, but it is much harder to translate those insights into daily habits. A renowned Brother at my Catholic high school explained this problem, this fundamental human limitation, in his discussion of the Eucharist. He was fond of exclaiming that, "if you really believed," you would crawl to the altar weeping. His point was not to say that no one actually believes in the Eucharist, but instead to point out the infinite gap between our actions and our beliefs. It would be easy to say that this makes us hypocrites or not true believers, but the truth is much more complicated. The idea of solidarity is similar. When we explore what it actually means, we learn as much about ourselves, our hopes, and our limitations as we do about the world around us.

Don

In his epic novel *The Death of Ivan Ilych*, Leo Tolstoy tells of the last struggles of a prosperous but doomed middle manager in the civil service of czarist Russia. Ivan Ilych is a conventional man who has led a conventional life. He has risen through the ranks of the bureaucracy to a position of respect. He has married well and is devoted to his wife, though the fire of their love has long been extinguished. He is the father of a soon-to-be-married daughter and a small son who adores him. As far as his neighbors and friends can see, Ivan has been successful. But Ivan is not well. Though unwilling to admit it even to himself, he fears he may be dying, and indeed he is.

None of his doctor's many treatments can halt the steady growth of the tumor that has invaded his body. Nor can the frequent visits of his parish priest keep at bay the fear that metastasizes in his soul. *The Death of Ivan Ilych* is the story not of an event, a happening to which an hour and a minute can be assigned as on a death certificate; it is the story of a journey into darkness and finally into light, a journey that continues unrelentingly in the face of all resistance until, in the end, time dissolves into eternity.

Tolstoy skillfully describes the sufferings of Ivan. Anyone acquainted with death will find his description quite convincing, even chilling in its familiarity. But Tolstoy is especially shrewd in assigning as the cause of Ivan's most intense suffering not the physical pain that he must constantly endure but rather an inner torment of the soul that arises in a kind of spiritual resistance. This resistance keeps Ivan poised on the brink: hovering between life and death, between heaven and hell, between peace and pain,

between torment and salvation. And the sharp point of this ful-
crum, upon which he is firmly impaled, is his inner conviction
that his life has been just and that there is nothing for which he
must make amends.

The conviction of his own righteousness in the face of death
and before God has him stuck, and from there springs his deepest
agony. Ivan imagines being grabbed by unseen hands that snatch
him up and stuff him into the mouth of a black sack, only he
never quite goes into the sack. He hovers there able neither to go
in nor to back out. His entrance is blocked by his refusal to let go
of his self-justification. His escape is blocked by the certainty of
his impending death. Ivan is held fast there at the mouth of the
sack, at the edge of darkness, between life and death.

By now he is delirious, as full of morphine as of pain, and
nearly oblivious of his surroundings. At the moment when all
seems lost, something happens that causes him to abandon his
relentless and unconvincing self-justification. His young son has
come up to his deathbed. He places his small hands in those of
his father's and kisses him. That touch sent Ivan tumbling into
the sack. It was in that act of grace that his life was saved. At that
moment he gave up the foolish claim that his life had really been
all right and that he himself had made it so. Then he accepted
that he could no longer save himself, no longer answer before
God for the rectitude of his behavior. In that very instant Ivan
stopped suffering. His physical pain continued, and after a few
moments of searching he could locate it again and feel it, but it
had completely lost its terror for him. From then on he became
indifferent to his pain, because his real suffering had ceased and
his true joy begun. Ivan discovered in the final moments of his
life one of the most pervasive, yet elusive, of all truths: we are
gifts to each other. Ivan's son, with the tender touch of a young
child, gave his dad what had always evaded him.

To see and appreciate every person, including our vulnerable
sisters and brothers, as gifts and not as burdens was the stance of
one of my heroes, Pope Paul VI. In 2012 Pope Benedict XVI
named him as a person of heroic virtue, granting to him the title
of Venerable for the exemplary way he embraced life. In the year

before his papal election, 1962, he journeyed to South Africa, where he participated in the groundbreaking ceremonies for the Maria Regina Mundi church in the black district of Johannesburg, ignoring the apartheid laws of the time. He would go on to become the most traveled pope in history up to that time, journeying to six continents, reaching out to the poor and raising his voice to advocate for justice everywhere he went. In the summer of 1978 Pope Paul VI could sense that his life's journey was coming to a close. He would live out his final weeks at the papal summer residence at Castel Gandolfo. There he began to compose a sort of last will and testament. Since he personally possessed no treasures of this world, he had only spiritual insights from his own experiences. He wrote, "As for me, at the end I would like to have a recapitulating and wise vision of the world and of life. I think this vision should be expressed in gratitude. Everything was gift, everything was grace. And how beautiful was the panorama that we traversed."[20]

Never before in human history have so many of us chosen to travel in order to be enriched by the beauty and goodness we encounter in each other at our destinations. Paradoxically, at the same time, never before have so many persons been forced to travel outside their place of origin by circumstances that are intolerable, often inhuman. In our day millions of persons are pushed out of their homelands by deadly violence, unimaginable economic privation, and the constant search for food and security. In the last three decades the number of people on the move has actually doubled from approximately 100 million to now nearly 200 million people. That represents one out of every thirty-five persons alive in our world today. We have become a people on the move, drawn by choice and by painful circumstances beyond our control.

In the summer of 2004 I shared an adventure with four of our seminarians enrolled at St. Mary Seminary in Cleveland, Ohio, where I had been teaching moral theology for two decades. We had an opportunity to volunteer at Nyumbani, the first hospice for HIV-positive orphans in Kenya, and to work at the Children and Life Mission in Uganda, a home run by Good

Samaritan sisters for former street boys rescued from the street violence in the capital city Kampala. The seminarians were able to meet and befriend some young people whose lives had been lived out in extremely vulnerable conditions. It was a life-altering experience, and the world looks different now to each of us.

It was wonderful to see the transformation in these four seminarians. The most recurring reflection given by each of them was that this opportunity to see and touch a distant part of our world was a gift. It remained so, even when this adventure placed them near suffocating poverty. A leader among them, Mike Denk, wrote, "I would never be able to see myself the same, the world the same, or my obligation to care and provide for those who are most poor and vulnerable." Mike's first experience of being with extremely vulnerable persons triggered a powerful response within him that could never have been anticipated. Reflecting back on the impact of that experience, Mike shared with me some of his reflections:

> When I entered the seminary in 2001 I had no idea that I would embark on a journey that would take me across the world. I went to the seminary with the notion that I was giving my life to God and so all adventure would come to an end. What I discovered is that when we draw close to God and offer him our lives he takes us places beyond our wildest dreams.
>
> It is now nearly a decade later and the children of Africa have always held a piece of my heart. I still tell the stories, I still relish in the memories, but most importantly I have been formed as a priest and as a person with a heart for the poorest of the poor. I had been repeatedly warned that taking a mission trip such as this would be a life-altering event; still I could never have imagined how much my life would be impacted by this initial trip.

The most profound changes were also the most surprising ones. Not only did the physical world around him appear different, so did the realm of the spirit and his appreciation of who

Jesus is. The very way Mike prayed to God changed because of memorable encounters he had with God's children that summer. In his journal he would write,

> There are two scripture passages that have not left my mind since our memorable trip to Africa. The first is Jesus inviting Peter to touch him—"put your hand into my side" (John 20:27) so that you may believe. I have been given the opportunity to place my hands into the side of Jesus, to touch the wounded and broken, to experience more the mystery of suffering and vulnerability.
>
> The second passage is "the harvest is plenty, but the laborers are few" (Matt. 9:37). Father Joseph Valente, a Comboni missionary from Italy ministering among the street youth in Kampala, gave a homily to us on our last Sunday morning in Africa. That very night he had a fatal heart attack. We were struck with the realization that we were eyewitnesses to his final reflections on the words of Jesus. He centered all his thoughts on this very passage. He imaged the harvest Jesus spoke of as the children that were in abundance in the streets. He saw how they were wasting away because there was no one there to gather and care for them. I've realized since this trip that around the world the harvest is abundant; there is an abundance of vulnerable children throughout the world just waiting to be helped and held by us. These gifts are so pure and wonderful. These children are sent from God, created by God, given to us by God, and they are being wasted. They are perishing in the streets because they are not loved; they are not seen as a gift but a burden. I have been given this opportunity to see their goodness, I have been able to see the wonderful gifts that they are, I have been able to touch the side of Jesus when I touch them, and I thank God for them.

The children of whom Mike wrote would flock to Father Valente in droves, reminiscent of how the youth felt drawn to Jesus and just yearned to touch him. Father Valente literally saved the lives of scores of street children in Kampala who lived in peril from the dangers that haunt them: hunger, disease, and the violence that was a part of their daily routine on the streets or in the homes they fled. He brought them to the Children and Life Mission at Namugongo, outside the capital city, where they were protected and nurtured by caring adults. He saved them from another, equally perilous fate: too many of these kids have lost a sense of their own dignity. The affection and selfless love of this elder son of Italy for the young sons and daughters of Africa empowered them to see themselves in a whole new light. What Father Valente saw is what all humanity must come to see: our young embracing life with the joyful innocence innately their own.

From my own travels I have been struck by how the youngest generation in the human family longs for all the same things, no matter where they live. Whether one is growing up in America's farmlands, inner cities or suburbs, or in the huts and villages of Africa, or in one of the massive urban centers of Asia in Tokyo, Shanghai, or Mumbai, our children all seek love, acceptance, joy, and a chance to reach the future. The writer Ina Hughs composed one of my favorite prayers. She takes me in my moral imagination to those far away that I care for deeply. Are our hearts big enough, our spirits noble enough, to embrace all humanity? Can we have our hearts expanded?

We Pray for Children

Who sneak popsicles before supper,
Who erase holes in math workbooks,
Who can never find their shoes

And we pray for those
Who stare at photographers from behind barbed wires,
Who can't bound down the street in a new pair of sneakers,
Who never "counted potatoes,"
Who are born in places we wouldn't be caught dead,
Who never go to the circus,

Who live in an x-rated world.
We pray for children
Who bring us sticky kisses and fistfuls of dandelions,
Who hug us in a hurry and forget their lunch money.

And we pray for those
Who never get dessert,
Who have no safe blanket to drag behind them,
Who watch their parents watch them die,
Who can't find any bread to steal,
Who don't have any rooms to clean up,
Whose pictures aren't on anybody's dresser
Whose monsters are real.

We pray for children
Who spend all their allowance before Tuesday,
Who throw tantrums in the grocery store and
pick at their food,
Who like ghost stories,
Who shove dirty clothes under the bed and never
rinse out the tub,
Who don't like to be kissed in front of the carpool,
Who squirm in church or temple and scream in the phone,
Whose tears we sometimes laugh at and whose
smiles can make us cry.

And we pray for those
Whose nightmares come in the daytime,
Who will eat anything,
Who have never seen a dentist,
Who aren't spoiled by anybody,
Who go to bed hungry and cry themselves to sleep,
Who live and move, but have no being.

We pray for children
Who want to be carried and for those who must,
For those we never give up on and for those who

don't get a second chance.
For those we smother . . .
And for those who will grab the hand of anybody
kind enough to offer it.
Ina J. Hughs[21]

Notes

[1] John Stott, *The Cross of Christ* (Westmont, IL: IVP Books, 2006), 303.

[2] See Fyodor Dostoevsky, *The Brothers Karamazov,* esp. book 5, chapters 3 and 4 ("Rebellion" and "The Grand Inquisitor") (New York: Farrar, Straus and Giroux, 2002).

[3] The best statement of this doctrine can be found in St. Augustine's *On Free Choice of the Will* (Indianapolis: Hackett, 1993).

[4] Hannah Arendt, *Eichmann in Jerusalem: A Report on the Banality of Evil* (New York: Penguin, 1994).

[5] Pope John Paul, "On Social Concerns," December 30, 1987, http://osj. webaloo.com/files/officeforsocialjustice/files/Solicitudo%20Rei%20Socialis. pdf.

[6] Ibid.

[7] Father Placido Fonseca, *Tracks* (n.p., 2007), 88–89.

[8] Ibid.

[9] Ibid., 20–21.

[10] Susan Wolf, "Moral Saints," *Journal of Philosophy* 79, no. 8 (1982): 419–39.

[11] C. S. Lewis, "The Abolition of Man," in *The Abolition of Man* (New York: HarperCollinss, 2001), 53–81.

[12] Robert Wachbroit offers a similar insight in his essay, "Genetic Encores: The Ethics of Human Cloning," in *Biomedical Ethics*, 7th ed., ed. David DeGrazia and Thomas Mappes (New York: McGraw-Hill, 2010), 583–89.

[13] In his illuminating article, "Even If It Worked, Cloning Wouldn't Bring Her Back," Thomas H. Murray makes a similar observation about the purpose of cloning Michael Jordan; in DeGrazia and Mappes, *Biomedical Ethics*, 580–83.

[14] See Michael Sandel, "Mastery and Gift," in DeGrazia and Mappes, *Biomedical Ethics*, 610–14.

[15] The Serenity Prayer is sometimes attributed to American theologian and ethicist Reinhold Niebuhr (1892–1971).

[16] *Tracks*, 60.

[17] Wes Moore, *The Other Wes Moore* (New York: Spiegel and Grau, 2011).

[18] *Tracks*, 73.

[19] Plato's *Meno* is a Socratic dialogue that famously tackles the question of whether virtue can be taught. See *Five Dialogues*, trans. G. M. A. Grube, 2nd ed. (Indianapolis: Hackett, 2002), 58–92.

[20] Donald Hanson and Donald Dunson, "Surrendering to Grace: The Deaths of Ivan Ilych and Paul VI," *Emmanuel* 105, no. 6 (July/August 1999): 358–61. The original source of the quote is a work in French by Daniel Ange titled *Paul VI: Un Regard Prophetique,* vol. 2 (Editions Saint-Paul, 1979), 343–51. The translation as appears in *Emmanuel* is an original translation by Sister Edith Turpin, OCD, Carmel, Covington, Louisiana.

[21] Printed in Marian Wright Edelman, *The Measure of Our Success* (New York: William Morrow, 1993), 95.

Afterword

Over the course of this book, it might seem that we have succeeded only in making the idea of solidarity more complicated. If every approach to this question is seriously flawed, what has been the value of a philosophical reflection? Don't we risk undermining the fervent belief that we do, indeed, have obligations to others, even if we cannot fully articulate them? If philosophical reflection is often painful and inconclusive, then what is the point?

One intuition might be to forswear philosophical reflection and opt instead for a leap of faith. Once we recognize the limits of our philosophical understanding and appreciate how complicated human beings really are, we might be tempted to stop thinking and simply believe. Maybe faith alone will guarantee the righteousness of our action, regardless of our own understanding. After all, Matthew 18:3 tells us the following: "Truly I tell you, unless you change and become like little children, you will never enter the kingdom of heaven." Maybe the lesson is to give up philosophical reflection and attempt to live like children, who simply accept on faith alone that we must care for one another. A corollary to this idea is that it is better to live in the moment, to embrace the duty to others when we see it, rather than adopting the critical distance necessary for understanding our moral obligations. After all, it is much easier to experience love than to define it, and the lack of a coherent definition does not mitigate the experience.

If something is mysterious about the idea of solidarity, that does not free us from the obligation to make sense of it. Reflecting on its meaning can provide a moral check on behavior that purports to be genuine, when in fact it is rooted in selfish motives or disrespectful of those it claims to help. The problem with this interpretation of the famous passage in Matthew is that children, like all human beings, make mistakes when they think they are doing good deeds. Becoming childlike is not an injunction to be naive, but rather to have the humility not to presume to know the answer and the intellectual curiosity to ask why things are the way they are. It is to be curious rather than cynically skeptical.

A childlike realization of a simple truth takes a lifetime to digest and make one's own. A classic favorite statement of the difference between the wisdom of the old and the wisdom of the young is found in an example from G. W. F. Hegel's supremely challenging work, *The Encyclopedia Logic*. The old man can "utter the same religious sentiments as the child, but for [him] they carry the significance of his whole life. Even if the child understands the religious content, it still counts for him only as something outside of which lie the whole of life and the whole world."[1] The old man's advantage over the child is an entire lifetime of self-reflection. Although this can be painful and at times inconclusive, it is the prerequisite for building strong moral character. It also seems like a key ingredient in fostering an authentic ethic of solidarity, since this moral goal assumes we are raising consciousness and not just cash.

Just because we do the right thing does not mean that we have sufficiently examined the beliefs behind those actions. As William Clifford warned us earlier, we can be "heretics in the truth." How can we expect consistently to act rightly if we do not bother to reflect on what makes an action moral? If we neglect to examine our beliefs, we can still, at times, make morally good choices, just like the child can act right without really understanding why. But that does not free us from the responsibility of examining our lives and our very identities to better understand our moral obligations to others.

Even Blaise Pascal, a great defender of religious faith," presents his view as a thought experiment. For Pascal, having faith is not an invitation to stop thinking, but a reminder to soften our hearts so that we can be open to a faith that defies logical explanation. Catholics have a special reason to reflect on the meaning of their beliefs: Catholic theology (from St. Augustine to St. Anselm and St. Thomas Aquinas) consistently stresses the unity of faith and reason. If the proper Catholic attitude is "faith seeking understanding," then it is at least misguided, and possibly immoral as well, to ignore the philosophical challenges that accompany a life of faith.

It is worth asking whether we can ever truly avoid thinking about our deepest convictions. Once we are old enough to think for ourselves, can we ever truly shut off that remarkable faculty? Doubt, in some form or another, seems inevitable, as human beings are constantly asked to give an account of why they believe what they believe. Isn't it better to have exerted the mental and emotional effort to get clear on why we hold our deepest commitments so that we are prepared when doubt sets in? Whether we are asked to answer to ourselves or to others is irrelevant. We can, at times, be our own harshest critics.

While it is true that reflecting on one's commitments risks undermining them, this same act of reflection insulates these beliefs from the doubts and criticisms that inevitably arise. It is also what gives our moral beliefs true and lasting value. Is there a single religious belief that is better off unexamined? Take, for instance, the idea of tithing. Someone could easily write a check for 10 percent of his or her salary, but tithing implies much more than a simple donation. It is an act of self-sacrifice that takes on a spiritual dimension. Someone who tithed without reflecting on it would misunderstand the whole point of the practice (would they even be tithing?), since anyone can give 10 percent but only believers can truly tithe. Another example is the role of Christian apologetics in the modern world. How are true believers to combat the arguments presented by the so-called New Atheists (Richard Dawkins, Christopher Hitchens, Sam Harris, et al.) if they have not thoughtfully considered their own beliefs?

The critical examination of one's beliefs might also be regarded as a proper use of freedom: for what other purpose is the gift of free will? As we have seen, Ivan, Dostoevsky's character, savagely mocks the idea of creating a people weak and free. What better response do we have to Ivan's objection but to say that genuine beliefs (including faith in God) are thoughtful, freely pursued, and worthless otherwise? If God were content with an uncritical acceptance of truth, He would have created humans to be moral robots. What could possibly justify all the evil wrought by free will, except to say that freedom is the condition for having any genuine beliefs at all? To rob us of freedom would be to make us, as we know ourselves, extinct.

The failures of each approach that we considered are instructive and productive rather than absolute. For instance, even though some attempts at solidarity are distorted by emotional appeals, it does not follow that empathy plays no role in genuine solidarity. The crucial role it plays can only be understood once we have seen the difference between its legitimate and illegitimate use. To say that our failure to understand is productive suggests that we can make progress in articulating our own moral beliefs. But we can do this only by understanding the limits of each approach to solidarity. Much like the Serenity Prayer asks us to contemplate what is in our control and what is not, we cannot understand our commitments unless we know what they entail and what they do not.

In the manner of the renowned Greek philosopher Socrates, we first have to "know what we do not know." This wisdom frees us from making absolute claims and allows us to recognize partial and limited, but important, truths. Yes, moral argument is an important way to comprehend what it means to be in solidarity with someone we might never meet. But its fatal flaw is its inability to motivate not just theoretical but *practical* agreement. Yes, personal experience is an important element in cultivating a genuine ethic of solidarity. But personal experience that is not constantly brought to mind becomes a set of quaint stories, interesting anecdotes, and photographs propped up on a desk.

Undertaking this sort of spiritual exercise is a way to cultivate not just a live heart but a live mind as well. Armed with beliefs that seem devout but are actually superficial, dogmatists never develop an appreciation for the complexity of human experience. But this means that they also lack important moral and intellectual virtues that can be acquired only in the messy process of sorting out one's beliefs and commitments. Consider the political virtue of toleration: The ability to *understand* what one's fellow citizens believe without actively endorsing that belief is the mark of a sophisticated mind. It requires a critical distance from one's own beliefs and a good deal of moral imagination to project oneself into another's shoes. It is tempting to say that those other beliefs are simply wrong (without making the effort to understand them) or to say dismissively that people are free to believe what they want (again with no effort to understand what they believe). But toleration is a crucial virtue in a democratic society (where citizens have very different ideas about the good life) precisely because it can bring people together without impeding their freedom.

Another good example is the value of learning a foreign language. Even if one never visits the country whose language one is learning, though clearly that would be preferable, the direct confrontation with what is unfamiliar helps to build a strong mind. Learning that different cultures have different ways of talking about the same concept makes for a nimble mind and a more flexible personality. One day a representative of the study abroad program visited Jim's freshman seminar class. She asked the students why they might not consider going abroad. Many of the answers were predictable (e.g., concerns about safety, funding, and more). One student offered a unique response. He said, "Why would you travel anywhere else if you already have everything you need?" This answer is interesting for several reasons: If you have nothing with which to compare your experience, how would you know if you have everything you need? How do you know whether you even understand what you *need* until you are put in a situation where that concept means something very different for you?

If we do not reflect on our beliefs, our minds will not be sharp and our capacity for moral imagination will be diminished. Out intellectual and moral growth will be permanently stunted.

But even though philosophy is the enemy of dogmatism in all of its forms, it does not necessarily undermine all of our beliefs and leave us empty-handed. There is an enormous difference between a conclusion that is accepted uncritically and a conclusion achieved as a result of thought and effort. The invitation to stop thinking and simply believe is analogous to a math teacher letting a student skip the geometric proof and just copy the answer. The Pythagorean Theorem does not need this particular student to prove it, but this student needs to prove the Pythagorean Theorem. Otherwise nothing is ventured, nothing gained, nothing learned. We are not moral robots, and the world around us is as complicated as we are. So we should not be surprised if the conclusions of our philosophical and theological reflections are complicated, too.

Notes

[1] G. W. F. Hegel, *The Encyclopedia Logic*, trans. T. F. Geraets (Indianapolis: Hackett, 1991), § 237Z.